Dr Lyons -

I hope you enjoy! It is my honor to know you are reading this.

Though we met only briefly years ago, I hope we will meet again!

Please accept my late, but sincere condolences for the passing of Mrs. Lyons

Hang in there —
your friend
Randy Barnhouse
" Hambone "

"Dear Samuel Clemens"...
Message In A Bottle

Letters to Samuel Clemens

by: Randy Barnhouse

"Dear Samuel Clemens"...
Message In A Bottle

Letters To Samuel Clemens

Copyright 2017 Randy Barnhouse

ISBN: 9780692990919

with

Sea Dunes Publishing House
Melbourne Beach, Florida

Cover: Stacey Wright Photography, LLC
Samuel Clemens on cover: Lester Goodin
Continuity with cover and art: Seajay Milner
Editor: Sam Milner

OTHER BOOKS FROM SEA DUNES

Morris (Boots) Atkins...   "Family First"
    "Family First Reunion"   "The Set Up"

Carl Fismer and Sam Milner...
"Uncharted Waters"...The Life And Times Of Captain Fizz

"Man Overboard"...Captain Fizz and the Treasure Bizz.

Nan Vehorn Milner..."Rhymes...Recipes...Remnants"

Randy Barnhouse... "Dear Samuel Clemens"...
                                Message In a Bottle

Sam Milner... "Trouble With Treasure"
    "Double Trouble With Treasure"
    "Between Waters"
    "Beyond The Last Resort"
    "Treasure Of Indian Isle"
    "Tales Of The Treasure Coast"
    "Song Weaver"...Short Stories With Songs
    "Matanzas"...A St. Augustine Saga

Dedication...

To our war dead and combat veterans.

Foreword

During the past five years, I've had the opportunity to investigate several historical sites. One, is a Mississippi riverboat wreck near my home in Cape Girardeau, Missouri. The other is the Mark Twain Boyhood Home located in Hannibal, Missouri. The articles I've recovered have led me down a path where I have linked coincidences, facts and parallels which exist between all of the historical sites I've worked, including the Spanish galleons, Atocha and Margarita...which were discovered near the Marquesas, and the shipwrecks of the 1715 Spanish treasure fleet which lie off Florida's "Treasure Coast".

I hope you enjoy my method of tying the sites together and telling their histories as I relay my findings to Mark Twain via "bottle-grams", messages I have placed inside bottles and tossed into the Mississippi River in hopes of someone recovering them and contacting me. Samuel Clemens and Mel Fisher are at the core of these messages.

Tonight, as I end my seventh expedition, I write from the courtyard of Mark Twain's Boyhood Home in Hannibal, Missouri. Beneath Samuel Clemens' old bedroom window, I've recovered a wide variety of artifacts. The images contained within this book feature artifacts and treasure I've recovered over the past thirty-five years.

Treasure hunters take great risk investing their time, resources and safety into bringing to light amazing objects destined to be lost forever, were it not for their passion, patience and perseverance.

So...join me as we journey back into history.....Sam awaits.

Randy Barnhouse
September 30, 2017
Hannibal, Missouri

5

TABLE OF CONTENTS

Dear Mr. Clemens,

I hope this message makes its way to you and also hope you don't consider my correspondence a bothersome enterprise.

I'm Randy Barnhouse. Most of my friends call me Hambone...it's an old family nickname given to me by my sweet departed mother, Bernice. It seems that the first word I uttered was Hambone. I guess other nicknames could be worse! I am fond of it and it **does** fit. I consider myself fortunate my first word was Hambone rather than P-Brain, or something more unbecoming. I suppose in some circles the name Hambone is silly, but the name has served me well for 59 years. Mr. Clemens, as far as I'm concerned...I don't care what you call me...as long as you call me for supper!

Boyhood home...pre-1880's, Sam's old bedroom is window on top floor rear.
Photo: public domain

The reason for my intrusion is to share with you a recent turn of events that involves me, as well as you. I've been invited to survey the grounds of your boyhood home in Hannibal, Missouri with a metal detector. The purpose of this investigation is an attempt to find something; whether it be of metallic, ceramic or organic composition that can be identified as having been lost or discarded during the time frame of your residence there. Any discovery, whether it be buried or hidden and linked to you and your family would be a big deal. Your humor, fame and wisdom live on into the twenty-first century, and I suspect...will carry on through the ages.

A responsible metal detector operator, such as myself, seeks permission from the landowner before searching and digging holes. Although I do have permission from the administrators of the home, I come to you in order to obtain your blessing and maybe get a little guidance from you during our earthly project.

As I mentioned, you're still a huge figure today. When a discovery is made and linked to you, people will gather to "ooohh" and "aaahh" over it. They will point, admire, photograph and cherish

Boyhood home

the simplest artifacts, yet unknown to the world, that were possessed by Samuel Langhorne Clemens, better known as...Mark Twain.
In your comic story, **"Eve's Diary"**, you wrote, "If there wasn't anything to find out, it

would be dull. Even trying to find out and not finding out is just as interesting as trying to find out; and I don't know but more so." **This is exactly how I feel about the search for artifacts we're conducting at your boy-hood home...artifacts directly linked with you. Hopefully...you feel the same way too. When something in particular is found at the site it will be most interesting, indeed. Whether I succeed or fail, the journey will be a win-win situation. I learned long ago, any treasure hunter has to keep in mind they'll be pleased, no matter the outcome. The hunt must be just as satisfying as the gilded objects searched for.**

Sam, if I may address you in an informal way, my method of delivering letters to you will be considered unorthodox by most, as well as myself. If a wisp of you still occupies our world, I believe you will be in several places. Your earthly presence might tramp in Hannibal, Hartford, India or along the banks of the mighty Mississippi River itself. There are other places where your spirit may roam but I think the fore-mentioned places are the most important to you.

Cape Girardeau wall mural...
Thomas Melvin Studio

I live on the Mississippi River in Cape Girardeau, Missouri. As a riverboat pilot you sailed past our fair city many times. In, "Life OnThe Mississippi", you wrote..."Cape Girardeau is situated on the hillside and makes a handsome appearance." **You also wrote...**"There was another college higher up on an airy summit...a bright new edifice picturesquely and peculiarly towered and pinnacled...a sort of gigantic casters, with the cruets all complete." The odd building you described was the Third District Normal School, a state teacher training college. It burned on April 7, 1902. I have no idea whether the news of this tragedy reached you or not. Based on your description, if the news of the inferno did reach you, I feel you might have derived a bit of pleasure upon hearing it. I too, feel that the new school was a ghoulish, out of place structure. Your description was very kind. The Normal School lives on to this day as Southeast Missouri State University. I was awarded a degree as a teacher by the University in 1983. I have since retired from teaching in 2009.

Each letter I write to you will be sealed in a bottle and tossed into the mighty Mississippi. There are no post offices in heaven or hell, for that matter. Where we go, we never know until the last breath escapes our lungs. Maybe we disappear into inky oblivion from whence we came. Should your spirit dwell on the river, please read and respond in whatever manner a will o'wisp employs. I need your help while looking for your lost and discarded

Tossing a message at Cape Girardeau

possessions. Should you care to help in the venture, will you also guide my hand when corresponding. My talents are many, however...writing is not one of them. It seems that in our youth, most of us regard ourselves as great poets and writers. Yet to the young, reading is a painful pastime. In our older years we love a good book, yet writing is as painful to us as reading was in our youth. I do like to read...I am old. As my scribblings sail lazily with the current of Old Man River, their progress will be slow and maybe short-lived. The hindrances and dangers of the river you experienced as a pilot will become reality for the frail, paper-stuffed quart-glass containers. Snags, whirlpools, churning towboat propellers and other dangers may claim them. Perhaps, one will be found by a happy mudlarker searching the river's edge for treasures and in turn, contact me.

My old Cur, Barney...
sniffing out a message

What a thrill it would be to find a message in a bottle! I like to think as soon as I mail the bottles by tossing them into the river, the delivery to you will be instantaneous. Then, there would be no sorrow for the capsulated telegrams that end up as broken glass on the river bottom while bits of paper continue to float and find their way toward the Gulf. Goodnight, Sam. I'll mail this tomorrow. Hugs to Olivia and the girls...   Hambone

Dear Sam,

I haven't sent this message yet. I will be in Hannibal this week on the 16th, 17th and 18th to investigate the grounds of your humble home. How appropriate and timely it will be to launch the initial letter from there. This will be my second expedition to your boyhood home. The first one, in early August, produced results complete with recovered artifacts. The first experience in Hannibal was interesting, I must say. Events of the effort are the reason why this campaign of messages was conceived.

Allow me to share with you a true treasure discovery that happened almost 75 years after your passing. It's important that I tell you about it. The discovery beat Halley's Comet of 1986 return by a mere year. Close enough! A year on the cosmological time clock is an immeasurable fraction...an iota of a second.

On September 4, 1622, a fleet of 28 Spanish ships left Havana, Cuba en route to Spain. Several of the ships were treasure galleons. The galleons were loaded with gold, silver, copper, emeralds, jewelry and indigo loaded at the ports of Cartagena and Portobello. The Spanish King, Phillip IV, anxiously awaited the arrival of the flotilla of ships. His share of the treasure amounted to 20%, known as..."the royal fifth". King Phillip needed the assets to pay for Spain's role in the Thirty Year's War.

As the flotilla sailed to the northwest from Havana seeking the Gulf Stream's three to four knot current boost, the crew had to be concerned with the seas beginning to pick up in strength. By evening of the fifth, it was obvious to all passengers and crew alike, peril awaited them in the darkness. The external forces of wind, rain and hazardous currents steadily picked up, tossing the fragile wooden ships with hell-born will. Throughout the night and into the late morning of the 6th, all souls and cargo were sandwiched between the Grim Reaper and Davy Jones. The devout prayed, the crazed cursed and the livestock of cavalry horses, cows, and pigs filled the air with wailing guttural sounds, unbridled.

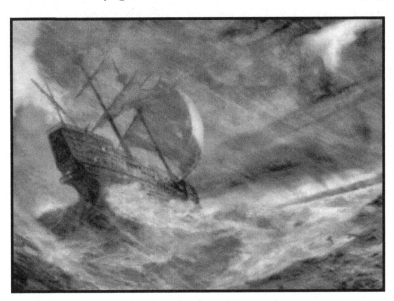

The Almiranta of the fleet, Nuestra Señora de Atocha, struggled in the rear of the convoy providing, by law, protection for the entire fleet. Her 20 bronze cannons were ready to take on any raiders who lurked at sea hoping to seize their $500 million in booty from the Atocha alone. Two hundred and sixty five souls were locked in the ship's hold in candlelit darkness. Sweat, screams, prayers, excrement and banshee-like howling winds was their final reality as they rode out their final minutes in the belly of the Atocha before she split apart; plank by plank, timber by timber, mast by mast. Relief from their floating purgatory did not come quickly.

On September 6, 1622, the Atocha...along with 260 souls was no more. It was reported by another ship in the Armada she was lifted by a monstrous green wave, driven onto the reef and foundered quickly. The plunge to the 60 foot depth where she rested was a suffocating death in icky blackness. The church officials aboard, along with crew, soldiers, passengers, slaves and peasants...were all as one. No praying, weapons, treasure, obedience, cursing or begging freed them from their common fate which was the same as the lamest squealing swine aboard. Five souls did survive the sinking; two black slaves, a seaman and two apprentices. It is notable to point out the lowest of the social and political caste were spared. Even the great explorer, Bartolome Garcia de Nodal, who in 1619 explored the passage between the Atlantic and Pacific Oceans and successfully rounded Cape Horn to the south of Tierra del Fuego, did not survive. It is assumed he drowned cowering in the darkened bowels of the Atocha. Though several attempts were made by the Spanish to locate and salvage the Atocha and her wealth, none were successful. Eventually, she was forgotten. The sediments propelled by ocean currents buried her, as did the opaque curtain of the mist of time. The Atocha was cast into archival history, stored away in the dark and dusty records of the Archives of the Indies in Seville, Spain. Fortunately, and because of that fact, she would live again in the modern world over three centuries later. When she lived again, the whole planet would know and revere her history and treasures. The men who released her from the depths would forever be entwined in her spell and a footnote in her history. I know this to be true, Sam. I, am one of the men who helped salvaged her in 1985. Halley was approaching, that silver comet portending the discovery of 52 tons of silver alone.

Sam, I'm tired and weary. I leave you now. This process takes effort and patience. I'm surprised I've made it this far. As I look back over my effort so far, I am pleased. Are you helping me? Did the glass and paper jetsam I hurled into the river in Hannibal last week reach you? In my next message I'll explain why the loss of the Atocha is important.

Thanks for being with me. Goodnight, Sam......

Hambone

Dear Sam,

Message two has been sailing it's way south since yesterday. I launched it from Cape Girardeau. The river stage was at nine and a half feet with the current flowing at a lazy two to three knots. The bottle was in view for a good while glinting in the late morning light, contrasted by a cinnamon-colored tide.

In, **"Life On The Mississippi"**, you wrote...*"Now and then we had a hope that if we lived and were good, God would permit us to be pirates"*. Diving for the treasures of the Atocha and bringing them to the surface for the first time since 1622 is as near the pirate life this old Missouri boy could have ever experienced. I owe the experience to one man, Mel Fisher...the undisputed king of sunken treasure...the discoverer of the Atocha on July 20, 1985.

The energy and wrath of the hurricane that opened up the sea's depth to swallow the Atocha was matched by the strength, courage, determination and persistence of Mel Fisher during his sixteen year search and discovery of her remains and rich cargo. Every doubloon, gold bar, piece of eight and treasure chest wrenched free of Poseidon's grip were freed to the surface with great sacrifice of life and treasure. Sam, like you, Mel and Deo Fisher suffered the unimaginable fate of losing a child, their first born son. Dirk Fisher drowned when his salvage boat turned over in the night at anchorage near the Atocha grave, July 20, 1975.

Angel Fisher...Dirk's wife, and diver...Rick Gage also died. Exactly a decade later, the final resting place of the main cultural deposit of the great ship was found by Mel's, "Treasure Salvors Incorporated". Mel's battle cry of, "Today's the Day", echoed across the water and radio every day for years. The day did come!.

Sam...you and Olivia, as well as Mel and Deo, could've given up on lofty goals upon losing your first born sons.

In 1872 you lost your son, Langdon, at the age of two. It was later determined that you might have taken him outside inadequately clothed for the weather conditions.

The Fisher's were riddled with guilt because of the loss of their son which was directly linked to the pursuit of their golden quest, which had also become Dirk's. Somehow, the matrimonial bonds of the Clemens and the Fishers survived intact. You completed the authoring of treasured literature and Mel discovered a treasured galleon. The world appreciates the treasured gifts you both contributed with resplendency.

The witching hour approaches, Sam. It's time to walk old Barney and head to bed. Sleep always comes quickly for me. Life is busy for this, supposedly retired, guy. In my next message it will become clearer why I'm writing to you along with chronicling the legend of Mel Fisher and the *Atocha*. My compulsion to do so dates back to my first visit to your boyhood home in Hannibal...the things I found, and the things I found out.

P.S...Are dogs there? That's where I want to go. Will Rogers said it best...

Hambone

Message Four...
"Digging Hannibal"
October 5, 2013
Cape Girardeau, Mo.

Dear Sam,

    Searching for and recovering items long-lost can be an intimate thing. This is especially true when looking for objects that were lost in the immediate vicinity of the demise of the souls who had possession of them. The artifacts and treasure of the Atocha shipwreck surrounded the unfortunate passengers and crew as they were rocked by the tempest and sent to the briny depths. After an initial phase of being allured by the golden and silver discoveries, I found the simple items from every day life were just as unique in their own way. They spoke to me. Candlestick holders were fascinating to find. How many meals did they grace a table for and who appreciated the glow of the stick they held, and for what reason were they gathered around it? How much laughter, conversation and arguing had the candlestick holders, with their fiery tube of wax and string, been witness to? Those ordinary things speak for humanity. The bullion and gemstones spoke for the sins of humanity. Wealth, greed, blood maligned faith and power adhered to the treasure as irremovable stains. Both classifications were intimate discoveries. One was a message from man, the other...a temptation from hell.

    Sam, to investigate and excavate the soil where you and your family once lived, loved and walked is an intimate act, too. What will your candlestick holder be that shines light on your time there on Hill Street? A coin, ring, shoe buckle, tool or an object that will be attributed to you? Knowing your affinity for buried treasure

20

causes me, in my wildest imagination, to hope that you buried something there.

On July 30, 2013...after a month's delay, I made my first expedition to Hannibal to begin the survey of your boyhood home. As I drove into the city, I remembered what you wrote about it in a letter to Alta, California to San Francisco Alta, California Newspaper on April 16, 1867. "Hannibal has had a hard time of it since I can recollect, and I was raised there. First, it had me for a citizen, but I was really too young to hurt the place."

In an 1887 letter to Jeanie Boardman you said..."I return like some banished Adam who is revisiting his half-forgotten paradise and wondering how the air and outside world could have ever seemed green and fair to him."

Sam...it was my first trip ever to Hannibal; as a starry-eyed fan, I drove toward the historic downtown area to find the Mark Twain Museum. I went inside, introduced myself to the person at the front desk and continued upstairs via the elevator to meet the director. I was warmly greeted and shown historic images of your boyhood home, as well as maps of the property. We left the museum and walked to your former residence on Hill Street. Along the way I took-in the sites of the historic area and then basked in the glow of history, of the streets you walked, and gazed at your playground...the mighty Mississippi River. I videoed the grounds of your boyhood home and asked questions pertaining to the project. My gracious hosts answered in great detail.

After checking into a nearby hotel, I decided to begin exploring the property. With my metal detector and other equipment in hand, I returned to your home with fair weather and four hours of daylight to spare. After walking around the property again, I picked the courtyard on the east side of your home to begin searching. After turning on the detector, laying out my notebooks, tape measure, GPS and probes...I whispered what I always say before I look for treasure...."Today's the Day!"....Mel Fisher's mantra and prophetic words motivated his treasure hunting crews to excitement and hope. The detector began beeping immediately on it's first pass over the soil. The first five holes I dug, where the detector indicated metallic content below the grass, contained nothing more than pull-tabs, bottle caps, modern nails and small bits of unidentified junk metal. At least I knew my machine was functioning well. With

Photo: Dominoc Genetti

fading daylight and a hungry, growling belly...I began to find coins. They were quarters, Sam...modern quarters. I found three of them. Each one had a letter on them in blood-red paint. Since I was running out of daylight, I didn't ponder the lettered coins very long. As I detected and dug other holes, I figured a "Twainiac Tourista" had written their initials on them in order to leave a kind of tribute. I found more scrap items before running out of time. I packed my equipment, walked up the hill to my hotel and muttered, "Tomorrow's the day!" I will find a trace of Twain.

After showering and stepping out for a late dinner, I returned to my room and unpacked all of the unidentified items I'd

Iron chips and fasteners

found, including the red lettered quarters. I tossed the quarters on the desk next to the window which allowed a perfect view of the Tom Blankenship home, a.k.a. Huck Finn's home. Two of the coins landed flat, red lettered side up. The letters were a **"D"** and an **"A"**. The third-quarter spun on the surface of the wooden desk and fell flat with its red lettered side down. With a magnifying glass I examined the rusty, crusty iron fasteners to make sure they didn't have any identifying marks or numbers. They did not. Then, I focused my attention on the crimson inscribed coins. I flipped over the third quarter revealing the **"Y"**. The quarters spelled out the word, **"D-A-Y"**! I immediately connected with, *"Today's the day!"* A tingle and a chuckle both struck me at once. I thought of Mel Fisher's words and asked aloud...*"Are you with me on this one Mel?"* What a great coincidence. Well, at least that's what I was thinking as I repacked my scrap iron and coinage booty. Little did I know in the coming days and weeks the discovery would put me

on a mysterious journey, one that would be obsessive and tiring. A voyage through the remarkable connections between you, Mel Fisher, the Atocha and a sunken Mississippi riverboat I'm investigating along the banks of the Mississippi River in my town, Cape Girardeau, Missouri.

More in next message, Sam. Time to turn in...

Hambone

Message Five...
"Dawson"
October 16, 2013
Cape Girardeau, Mo.

Dear Sam,

In, **"A Tramp Abroad"**, you wrote..."The church is always trying to get other people to reform; it might not be a bad idea to reform itself a little, by way of example."

In a letter to Henry Rigdon in 1905 you said..."Nothing agrees with me. If I drink coffee, it gives me dyspepsia; If I drink wine it gives me the tout; If I go to church, it gives me dysentery."

Your thoughts on heaven and hell leave me wondering whether you believed in an afterworld or possessed a noncommittal curiosity about heaven and hell. In your biography you wrote..."I have never seen what to me seemed an atom of truth that there is a future life...and yet...I am strongly inclined to expect one."

On June 1884's, **"Pudd'nhead Wilson Calendar"** page, your quote says..."When I reflect upon the umber of disagreeable people who I know have gone onto a better world, I am moved to lead a different life."

And finally in a letter to William Dean Howells on May 20, 1891 you wrote..."Travel no longer has any charm for me. I have seen all the foreign countries I want to except heaven and hell. I have only a vague curiosity about one of these."

I am inclined to believe you were on the fence, undecided, yet curious enough to lean toward believing in the ever-living soul, and if it becomes heaven or hell worthy as we tramp through our short presence during our physical existence on Mother Earth.

25

In my fourth message to you I ended with the story of the crimson lettered quarters that spelled part of the battle cry of Mel Fisher. In this letter I intended to elaborate on that remarkable find a bit more but something happened in Hannibal Sunday I was notified about which is as remarkable as the quarters found. In the first paragraph of this message your quotes concern religious belief, practice and an after-life. The discovery of the first bottle message to you is also wrapped in religious belief, practice, and maybe an after-life. The circumstance of the bottle discovery is as follows; Dawson, a young man living in Hannibal, found God at a spot on the bank of the Mississippi River. His newfound faith has led him out of addiction and has strengthened him for battles of a personal nature he's waging. He is strong, works at hard labor and feels for the first time in a long time...he has a chance. A true feeling of hope exists for this son of Hannibal. Dawson told me he is not quite up to being surrounded by people in a house of worship just yet. He prefers to go to the spot on the river where his Christian epiphany struck him. Last Sunday at his sacred spot on the river, Dawson found the first message in a bottle! Sam, when I launched the bottle, I tossed it into the river with all my might so it would not be snagged by the bank too quickly or get trapped in a swirling eddy. I watched it ride south with the current until I could no longer see it bobbing in the water. For whatever reason, it floated a few hundred feet, entered an opening in the levee and went aground at the spot near Bear Creek where Dawson found it at his personal place of worship. When Dawson called me to report the find on that beautiful Fall morning, he found me at the lake with my dog. I often refer to that lovely place as my church. How

26

better to commune with the Creator than in a natural setting of water, critters and fowl of every sort. Dawson was more excited about the meaning of the letter than finding a message in a bottle. He said he didn't think his faith could be more strengthened than the level of **that** which it was, but...the experience did just that. One line from the letter impacted him the most. "There are no post offices in heaven or hell, for that matter." According to Dawson, I was wrong about that. One has special delivery!

I observed a towboat heading up river the morning I threw it. After the towboat passed, I threw the bottle and thought of you during your piloting days on the river before the Civil War ended your time behind the wheel of many riverboats. The simplest explanation I can offer is, the wake from the boat and its barges pushed the bottle into the narrow opening in the levee and delivered it to Dawson. I'd like to think as soon as it hit the water, you read it and then forwarded it to him I have hopes the messages I deploy into the river will travel dozens, hundreds, and maybe even thousands of miles. I can't think of a better outcome for the first bottle found. The distance traveled is measured in yards, yet the meaning is measured eternally, at least to young Dawson.

Sam, you scribed a dedication for, **"Adventures of Huckleberry Finn"**, that wasn't used. You wrote..."To the once boys and girls who were comrades with me in the moving of the youth of antiquity in the villa Hannibal, Missouri. The book is inscribed with affection for themselves, respect for their virtue and reverence for their honorable gray hairs." Signed...the author.

While the introduction ended with a sample of your irreverent humor, the warmness you felt for the young men and women of your boyhood village is projected. I know you are pleased that Dawson found the message. Goodnight Sam...

Hambone

Dear Sam,

The discovery of the "lettered quarters" at your home impacted me enough to begin looking closely for other remarkable coincidences that might pop up. I didn't have to wait long for a flood of parallels between you and Mel Fisher to present themselves. For you to see the next parallel, I have to tell you another sunken boat story.

Last year in late September, I got a call from a friend of mine who had exciting news. While walking on the bank of the Mississippi River in Cape Girardeau searching for objects revealed by historic drought driven lows of the river, his wife had stumbled across a boat-wreck imbedded in the riverbank. He knew of my experience with wrecks from the Atocha days with Mel Fisher. He asked me if I'd take a look at the wreck. I quickly agreed to hike to the site and evaluate it. He said it looked old. My curiosity as a shipwreck-salvor made for an easy response. I agreed to go to the wreck-site and evaluate the boat and give my opinion as to its age and historical importance.

As I hiked up the river from the Broadway Levee gate to the wreck, my expectations of it being of historical importance were low. However, my excitement level was high. It was a hot, sunny day. The river was the lowest I'd seen it. The great 2012 drought revealed logs of every size by the hundreds on the banks of the Mississippi. Flotsam and jetsam of every type, size and color were mixed in with the hard, sun-dried mud along the banks of the

29

"Father of Waters". It was a mudlarker's dream for finding who knows what in the ebbing black ooze of sediment! When I spotted the landmarks my friend had described to me in his excited state, I made a precarious climb over the rocks to the edge of the river in

order to reach the location of the exposed wreck. What I found was remarkable. It was old and it was historic. The bones of a genuine sunken Mississippi riverboat of some age and sort was there at my feet. Before I left home to visit the wreck, I had packed a measuring tape, paper, pencil and a few screwdrivers for poking and prodding around the potential wreck. My phone provided me with a camera. These simple tools made it possible for me to record data.

Amy Grammer moments after discovering the wreck.
Photo: Russell Grammer

Before I began taking pictures, measuring, and doing a bit of prodding, I performed a visual of the site. What I had was an iron hull buried in the quagmire of mud. Only 25 feet of its length was exposed. What remained of it was buried in the riverbank. The level of the river was at 7 feet. I was able to walk around the perimeter of the boat with ease, even though at one point my foot became stuck in ooze. My shoe was sucked off as I pulled my foot out. At 5 foot intervals, wooden deck support-beams crossed the hull. Nails were embedded in the supports where the river had ripped away most decking. Some decking was still in place. Over the decades, fill... consisting of concrete blocks and rock, had settled on the wreck effectively pinning the decking

Don Greenwood sketching the wreck of the Amy Elizabeth.

and hull in place. A large iron cleat was still in place on the upper edge of the exposed hull. Underneath a massive chunk of concrete, a small hub was visible. The sediments filling the hull were a mix of bricks, concrete, rocks, glass, bottles and other things you might expect from years of flooding and deposits both natural and man-made.

Cross section of wreck

Wreck presentation.
Image: Russell Grammer

Russell Grammer and
prodigy students.

Russell and Amy Grammer realized the potential and immense
educational value the wreck held for their school.

The overall condition of the wreck was impressive. Any visible structure looked well preserved whether it was the wooden deck-supports or the hull itself.

After several hours of inspecting and recording rudimentary data, I made my way back up the rocks and began to hike back to the parking lot. I stopped at a bench and called my friend to tell him the wreck was very interesting and I wanted to do a further examination. I also told him we were obligated by law to apply to various local, state and federal agencies for permits to do any excavation on the site. All we could do on the site legally was to measure, photograph and research unless we had official clearance. I told him I would start the process if he'd like me to. He agreed. We both felt time was running short for any further examination. The river had revealed it and the river would reclaim it. Knowing how slow government bureaucracy works, I wondered how much of a chance we'd have to excavate and study the structure of the wreck and recover artifacts from its mud-filled bowels. It turns out that a

Holly Brantley of KFVS News...filming and interviewing students studying the wreck.
Image: Russell Grammer

year later, a connection between your boyhood home, the "lettered quarters", and this Mississippi boat-wreck exists. It's getting late, Sam. I will bottle this message and chuck it into the river tomorrow morning. Goodnight.....

Hambone

Greenwood's sketch of the Amy Elizabeth boat-wreck.

Dear Sam,

   I have pursued and studied the mystery of the Mississippi Riverboat wreck for over a year now. I'm pleased to say we've learned a lot about it, although...in the beginning, officials declared it to be a common tub of a barge not worthy of an archaeological investigation. Old Man River's currents and erosion from the passing wakes of tows and barges have stripped enough overburden from the boat revealing exciting details that have strongly indicated otherwise. The wreck is 70 feet long and around twelve feet wide. The hull is iron and the deck supports and decking are wood. Most interesting is that the wreck was not a common towed barge that would have been used to carry bulk cargo such as coal, rock, wood or other cargo not suitable for

being easily transportable overland other than by rail. This boat has a steering assembly complete with a rudder-shaft and connecting armature that joins to the mechanisms to move and steer with a rudder. Sam, it was self-propelled!

During the 2013 season we were able to confirm this due to erosion on the structure since late November, 2012, the last day I saw it before the river reclaimed her again for a nine month submersion.

In September of this year the river dropped to the required twelve-foot level allowing the first glimpses of her this year. The section not imbedded in the riverbank or covered over by mud, rock and sand is fully visible when the "Big Muddy" hits eight feet. During the past month the wreck was 90% revealed for a few weeks due to the lowest level of the river, being 8.5 feet. That's when we went back to work on her attempting to solve the mystery of her age and origin.

Another two huge discoveries were made this season. I found deck-trim running in an oval pattern across the deck that indicated where a wheelhouse wall joined the deck twenty feet forward of the stern and the newly affirmed steering assembly. Connected to the steering assembly was a flat plate rod

Measuring for the site-map

connecting the steering to the wheelhouse. The newly stripped muck from the river allowed us to find a conduit pipe. The iron pipe has wire sticking out of it with rubber and braided cloth-wrapped insulation. This wreck had some sort of an electrical system for powering lights for work or navigational purposes, or both. From my observation and research of the boat and its components, I have hypothesized that it was built in the time-frame of 1900 to 1920.

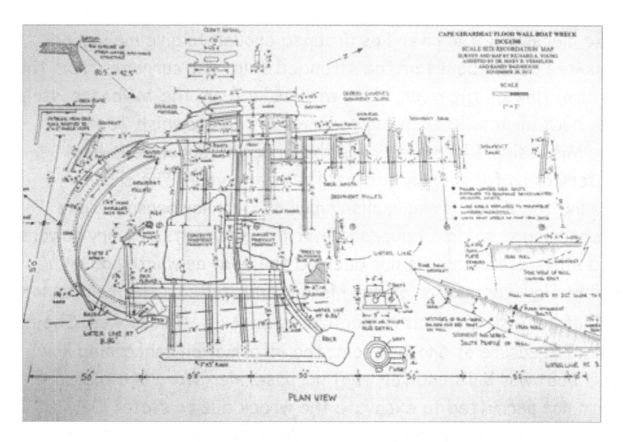

Scale site recordation map by: Richard A Young

The estimate of the date of its construction could change. Until I find other evidence, we'll go with the very early part of the 20th century. I find satisfaction in knowing there's a chance it plied the river trading, delivering and transporting. The comet, Halley, might have been seen in the sky and perhaps an imaginative glimpse of the great fireball by a river man on her deck thought of you astride it, spurring it like your Mexican Plug back into the blackness of the solar system.

Sam, in **"Mark Twain in Eruption"**, you wrote..."The Mississippi River will always have its own way; no engineering skill can persuade it to do otherwise." The river is definitely having its way with the wreck.

Like clockwork, the river has dropped enough to give me a good look-see of the bones of the stranded ship. The currents from the natural flow of the river, along with wake from the towboats, strip the boat of detail-obscuring sediments. The brownish water of the Mississippi River preserves the wreck, wrapping it in her watery arms for roughly ten months of the year. The erosion around the wreck is accomplishing what I cannot persuade any archaeologist to do. It appears that the occupants of ivory towers and state agencies have not deemed the boat as worthy of a scientific investigation of her history and content. Her hold is not full of gold, silver, gems and artifacts as Mel's, Atocha was. She is full of treasure of another sort, the information concerning how this boat was built and for what purpose. Her story is a treasure. I am not permitted to excavate the wreck due to state regulations. Thank God the river is doing the excavation for me. The river...is my trowel! When I was notified about the discovery of the wreck, it occurred to me this project could be an example of archeologists and treasure hunters working together for the common good of both. Such cooperation is needed! The battle between the two entities has been raging for decades. I have done my part as a treasure hunter for over a year now. My folder of the wreck is bulging with a site map, drawings, images, measurements and theories as to what she might be. All of the data is on deposit with the State of Missouri and our local museum. The wreck is not a common tub. It is a significant piece of our local and state river heritage. If it has to live on as an archival record as the Atocha did before it was fully examined and brought to the attention of the public to marvel and learn from...

Don Greenwood's initial artistic rendering.

then, so be it. This wreck is firmly embedded. It's not going anywhere!

In a letter to Orion and Jane Clemens on April 3, 1889, you wrote **this** about patience. "All good things arrive unto them who wait...and don't die in the meantime." I can out-wait the slow revelation of what the wreck is, Sam. I will stay at it. My name is forever linked with the documentation of this wreck. Should I pass before the mystery is solved, then I will join it in archival history. I will learn its secrets on the other side...right?

Two days after finding the lettered coins at your boyhood home, I was back in Cape Girardeau investigating the wreck. As expected, the river had dropped while I was in Hannibal and revealed the wreck for the first time of the 2013 season.

I was pleased with the effects of almost ten months of eroding under the watchful eye of "Old Man River". New structure was revealed that confirmed theories of structure and time frame of construction to some extent. Then, I noticed a bottle sticking out of the oozy odorous mud. It looked familiar. I'd seen one like it before.

The wind is picking up outside and a few distant rumbles of thunder can be heard down the creek. I need to batten down a few things and relieve 'ol cur, Barney. He is under my desk patiently awaiting. I'll pick up the story of the bottle in my next message. Goodnight, Sam...

Hambone

Message Eight...
"Message of a Bottle"
November 14, 2013
Cape Girardeau, Mo.

Dear Sam,

Today's been all right. I'm holding down the house with cur, Barney. Debra, my wife of 17 years, is in New Jersey visiting grandson, Leo. She left me with a full cupboard. I haven't starved in the absence of her cooking.

Today I studied the artifacts I've found so far in your yard of long ago. The two trips to Hannibal have been productive. Soon, I will fill you in as to what I've dug up.

I left you in message seven with the discovery of the bottle I found in the "Cape wreck". When I saw it I knew what it was before I pulled it from the muck. It was a Coca-Cola bottle, vintage 1923. It wasn't the first one of that make and year I've found around the site. It was the fourth one. In 1898 Colonel George Thilenius founded the Coca Cola Bottling Company at 228 North Pacific Street in Cape Girardeau. The bottles found on and near the wreck certainly didn't

sink with the boat. They, like the concrete and brick spoil covering the wreck, were cast into the river when no longer needed and ended up either on, or near the boat.

Each greenish-molded glass bottle was inscribed on the bottom in bold raised lettering, Cape Girardeau Missouri. They were fun to find and the patent dates on the bottles were close to the time frame of when our wreck was built. Unfortunately, this bottle was broken. Only the lower third of it was intact. Out of habit I looked at the bottom expecting to see the Cape Girardeau Missouri inscription. Crusty, dried mud covered the script, I spit on it and wiped away the crud. To my surprise it didn't say, Cape Girardeau. It read, Gary, Indiana. I stood there slightly puzzled wondering why it was from Gary and how it happened to settle on the wreck. After holding it in my hand for a minute, I returned the bottle fragment where I found it and turned my attention to details of the wreck which were a lot more interesting and of more importance than a Hoosier Coca-Cola bottle. As I went about my business measuring, photographing and recording other data, something bothered me about the bottle. I was sure that I knew someone from Gary, Indiana but I couldn't think of who it was. The entertainment group, "The Jackson Five", were from Gary...but I sure as hell didn't know them.

After gathering my belongings I left the wreck site very pleased with the new finds. As I walked south along the levee to the floodgate on Broadway, it occurred to me that Mel Fisher was from Indiana. Fresh in my mind was the memory of the lettered quarters I found only two days before. It was kind of a coincidence on some level. While the bottle was from Mel's birth state of Indiana...Indiana is a big state. I couldn't recall where in Indiana Mel was born, so I sat on a bench overlooking the Mississippi River and pulled out my smart phone. A quick search revealed Mel Fisher was born in Hobart, Indiana. The next search result made me sit bolt upright on my scenic perch. Hobart, Indiana is only 10 miles from Gary, Indiana and Mel and his family moved to Gary, Indiana when Mel was 12. He graduated from high school in Gary. I had barely taken-in the eerie revelation when another factoid hit me. Mel was born in 1922. The bottle was made in 1923. Interesting...very interesting coincidences. Forty-eight hours before, I'd been standing in your east yard in Hannibal marveling at the red scripted quarters that pushed my imagination to consider for a few relished minutes that Mel was giving me a sign he was there helping one of his "Golden Crewmen" on this day to find treasure..."Sam Clemens Treasure"...whether it be a choice artifact or historical data! From my repose above the rolling river, my imagination began to run freely again. The discovery of the bottle and quarters combined felt more like attention getting slaps rather than coincidences. I kicked my feet up on the concrete slab of the retaining wall in front of the bench and took-in the view of the river and the passing tows. I allowed myself more than a few minutes to dream and fantasize about the meaning and the delirious speculation I was entertaining. What should I tell Debra, or anyone for that matter? I'm sure that in some circles I'm already referred to as being eccentric, but to begin announcing to others what I'm contemplating beyond concurrence would be an act of self aberration. My closest treasure salvor friends would be the most receptive ear.

The finding of the bottle from Gary, Indiana on the Cape wreck, and the quarters from your home compelled me to be more perceptive to connections between you and Melvin A. Fisher. This was the moment. I didn't have to search long or deep to find them as you well know. From the first page of this packet of letters to now, I am revealing them. I will continue with the rest of the messages with more information.

What I found on the wreck that day wasn't a message in a bottle...it was the message of a bottle. Goodnight Sam...

Hambone

Message Nine...
"Comet Ison"
November 30, 2013
Cape Girardeau, Mo.

Dear Sam,

Happy Birthday, Sam! Missouri...the nation...and the world gained a favorite son 178 years ago today. While the entire planet admires and loves you, only Florida, Missouri can lay claim to you. Your taproot is buried in Florida. Your roots are in Hannibal. Your sturdy trunk is the Mississippi. The world is your branch. The fallen leaves are your literary works.

The Comet, Ison, is approaching the Sun. Last year the comet was 585 million miles away. Two days ago, at the speed of 850,000 miles per hour, Ison passed within one million miles of our Sol. The comet was slung around the sun and reemerged on the side from which it approached. We have been looking forward to viewing Ison on your birthday. Experiencing a comet during the time frame of your birth would be spectacular. Ison has been traveling from the Oort cloud toward us over a distance of several hundred million miles and is over four billion years old. It seems beyond coincidence the visit of this great, "dirty snowball", of a space traveler has arrived this last day of November, as you did.

This is one more event that comes from a mental and written list coming I draw upon for the substance of these messages. As Ison reemerged from the far side of the sun today, it appears to be in peril. The heat and solar wind it's been subjected to have taken their toll on the wayward mass of ice, gas and rock of which it is composed of. More than likely, our chances of seeing it fly back into the infinity of space has been greatly diminished, if not plain damn ruined! The pitiful remnants of what was to be the comet of the century will avoid our detection. It will pass by the earth like a raven in the blackest night, unseen, but there.

In your autobiography you wrote..."I came in with Halley's Comet in 1835. It is coming again next year, (1910), and I aspect to go back out with it. It will be the greatest disappointment of my life if I do not go back out with Halley's Comet."

"The Almighty has no doubt said...Here are these two unaccountable freaks. They came in together, they must go out together."

Sam, I notice you didn't mention being born or dying with Halley in the sky. You refer to your attachment as coming and going. "I came in," announces the arrival of an existing spirit. "I go out," infers an exiting as if "tally-hoing" to the next destination, not to a final resting place. How remarkable is it that in 1835 you arrived during the comet's appearance and left us in 1910 during the next Halley appointment, and the life and death off Ison arguably happened on your birthday? The odds are minuscule. They are notable. Beyond reality, they seem.

Although I'm disappointed Ison is no longer observable in the coming frigid December heavens, I'm content there was a comet for a few brief days coinciding with your birthday. Have my messages brought you back to us Sam? Did you hitch a ride on Ison for a visit? I wouldn't put it past you. You already know I'm wondering whether you helped us find the remains of the doomed Atocha during the 1986 visit of Halley. Have you read my messages and now you're communing with me to help me find treasure in Hannibal? The white vestments of Halley and Ison truly remind me of your iconic pearly suits.

Reading the above paragraph makes me realize sending these messages to you bring about mixed emotions to say the least. I have minor bouts of wondering about my sanity. Penning these letters sometimes feels like a journey into madness. This campaign of correspondence to a man long gone is haunting, outlandish, peculiar, curious and eccentric. But I continue on. To cease to continue due to an inner ominous turmoil isn't acceptable. To withdraw from my efforts of putting down on paper the remarkable coincidences I've spoken of would be a renouncement of historical parallels and a miserly act on my part. People who love Sam Clemens and Mel Fisher have a need and a right to hear this evidence as a collective group and to decide for themselves if these accounts are worthy of their time or trash as I hurl these messages into the river.

Goodnight, Sam...

Hambone

Dear Sam,

I must apologize for not having written for a few weeks. I had a technologic breakdown...my computer went on the fritz! Now, I'm back and running. I just returned from the river where I hurled a message to you. I watched it for a good while until the cold wind barreling down the Mississippi River Valley became unbearable and drove me to find warmth and shelter. Due to the continued drought, the Mississippi is at a low of 12.02 feet. The current is running fairly fast, carrying the bottle south at around five knots. Hopefully, you've read the message and sent it along its way. I look forward to hearing from the next river-comber who finds the message and contacts me. So far, I've only heard from a young man whose name is Dawson, a resident of Hannibal. I presume and expect anyone who retains a smidgen of curiosity and finds one of the messages I've tossed into the river will contact me and share with me the story of their consequence.

Sam, I must say your short visit to Key West on January 6 and 7, 1867 comes with a remarkable story of a stricken ship, deaths at sea and other remarkable parallels associated with you and treasure finder, Mel Fisher. Although your time in Key West took place nearly one hundred years before Mel's time, both of you were drawn to and landed on that magic island in grand style as characters in a saga of men and women struggling on doomed ships at sea.

When you departed San Francisco at noon, December 15, 1866 on the steamer, **America,** it was a lovely sunny day. Your makeover was complete. You had a new name. Samuel Langhorne Clemens had become the famed, Mark Twain. The past few years was a kaleidoscope of adventures, events and people, feeding your pen with fodder as you wrote about subjects which made readers world-wide look forward to your next masterpiece.

Your work, **"The Celebrated Jumping Frog Of Calaveras County"**, was published two years earlier on November 18, 1865 in The New York Saturday Press. From meager beginnings in the small town of Florida, Missouri...Monroe County...to world renown author, humorist and man of the world extraordinaire by the age of thirty two, is not only amazing...but necessary. Dozens of novels, hundreds of letters and innumerable stories still existed within your mind while waiting to be released and published on paper. We are thrilled and blessed with the prolific nature of your writing.

This trip to New York was intended to give you an opportunity to see family and friends before traveling around the world on the, U.S.S. Quaker City. Your book, **"Innocents Abroad"**, humorously chronicles the adventure that you referred to as your, "Great Pleasure Excursion." But first, you had to make it safely to New York.

Key West was not a scheduled port of call for the doomed passengers on the ship which you were about to sail. Those of you that made it to Key West were glad indeed to set foot on shore and distance yourself from the plague-ridden ship, San Francisco.

The first sign of trouble on the voyage happened when the America was raked by an unexpected storm. It was a brief but fierce gale forcing most passengers on deck, some of them to their knees in prayer for deliverance from the weather's tempest. The storm abated with no injury to the souls aboard nor destruction to the ship. I have to wonder if those who begged and prayed for mercy during the storm received divine attention as their words broke the silence on the decks and in the cabins of the ship, San Francisco, which you all sailed on from Greytown, Nicaragua on January 1, 1867.

The steamer, America, had discharged you on the Pacific port of Nicaragua. You enjoyed the trek across the Isthmus and wrote well of it. New York was still a long haul. However, the San Francisco would be the vessel to deliver you to your New England destination. You will make it to New York on January 11. Some of your fellow passengers will not. There is a price to pay to the San Francisco. Ships sometimes do that. They exact a price, a sort of sacrifice. It's in injury and death that we pay our well earned dues. The right boat on the proper sea gives us rich pleasure. When the bill comes due...it is paid, quickly and surely, and then...the clock begins again.

Asiatic Cholera hitched a ride in the small intestines of some of your fellow passengers and crew of the San Francisco when you left Greytown, Nicaragua. Not one of the afflicted souls had symptoms upon the departure. Those carrying the disease had ingested the villain one to five days before the sudden onslaught of symptoms and misery. On the second day of the voyage, cholera announced it's presence as a doctor pronounced its name. Two

50

passengers became sickened and died within hours, one in the evening, and the other around midnight. The Captain plotted and steered a new course to Key West for relief and medicine. The San Francisco herself had problems. Several breakdowns resulted in the ship rolling helplessly while the crew attempted repair. Heat, stench and misery shrouded the decks as the passengers remaining alive awaited their fate.

Sam, the new course plotted for the San Francisco caused your ship to pass near, if not directly over the bones and sunken treasure of the Nuestra Senora de Atocha! For nearly 245 years the great Spanish galleon lay in slumber. Your dream of finding treasure was practically beneath your feet, ten fathoms deep. All the treasure of the Atocha would have meant nothing at the time.

Three more passengers passed from the dreaded disease bringing the total carnage to five victims. The passengers and crew of San Francisco would have gladly given the millions in treasure that lie in the deep for safe passage to Key West.

Sam, if you recall...when the Atocha took her perilous plunge into the deep in 1622, she left only five survivors. During modern day salvage of her remains, five salvagers have been lost. During your ill fated voyage from Nicaragua to Key West, five of your fellow passengers were hastily shrouded and slipped over the side into the clear blue sea of the Florida Straits to eternal rest among the corals, shells and sea creatures.

All about the same time, a comet...which would not be officially discovered for another three months, hovered over this cholera catastrophe unfolding on Mother Ocean. Temple 1, will be discovered by Wilhelm Temple on April 3, 1867. The comet completes an orbit of the sun every 5.5 years. In 2005, our Space Agency...NASA, whacked Temple 1 with a high velocity space probe to investigate it. A 200 meter wide dimple is all the errant rock suffered. The scientists learned a lot of useful information from the cosmic collision.

By the Grace of God, Davey Jones, Poseidon...or hell...maybe all three, the scourged crew and passengers of the cholera infested San Francisco limped into Key West harbor on January 6, 1867. When your feet hit the dock in Monroe County, Florida that day...you were just as reborn as you were the day you were born in Monroe County, Florida, Missouri on November 30, 1835.

It's been a long day, Sam. I have a few things to tend to and a cur to walk. I'll pick this back up in message eleven. There is much more, Sam...much, much more. Thanks for being here. I'll mail this to you in the morning...if the river has good flow....

Hambone

Dear Sam,

The San Francisco, California newspaper, "Alta", published a letter from you on March 23, 1867. The letter was written on January 6, 1867. You scribed the letter in Key West after finally making it ashore and away from the death ship San Francisco. Evidently, the peculiarity of Cayo Hueso compelled you to record your observations within hours of your landing. Your time on the island will be brief. Leave it to you and your prolific nature in writing to quickly record the sights, smells and opinions of, "The Rock". When I found the letter tonight after hours of researching, I was thrilled. Before tonight I didn't know very much detail about your stay in Key West. This new information is already being mined for circumstances that link you and Mel. Interesting parallels are coming to light beyond what I've told you already.

Although I've found no record of what dock the crew and passengers of the San Francisco disembarked from, clues from your account of Key West have convinced me that you tied up at Key West's, Bight Harbor, which is an excellent harbor, as you described it. You said... "Fort Taylor, an immensely strong fortification, sits in the edge of the sea and commands the entrance to the harbor, but we did not visit it...the walk would have been too great." Had you docked at Mallory Square, you would have been very near the fort. Fort Taylor would have indeed been a long trek from Key West's Bight Harbor. You do give an account of the black people, their location and condition. You are describing present day Bahama Village in "Key Weird". If you ranged that far from Key West's Bight Harbor, I imagine your fatigue was great, especially after the trials on the stricken San Francisco. You were in close proximity to the Fort, another thirty minute walk would have taken you to it and it's grand design and history replete with cannons aimed out to sea.

On Sunday you attended services at St. Pauls Episcopal Church. Although your writings have not totally represented you as a full time man of faith, the harrowing sea voyage you had experienced in the days before this holy day led you back to be a man publicly demonstrating his faith. What did you pray for that day, Sam? Did you give thanks for deliverance from the reaper or ask for safe passage on the next leg of the voyage to New York? Were you a giver or a taker? Maybe both. St. Pauls church had it's first service on Christmas Day, 1832 in the County Courthouse on Jackson Square. The first incarnation of it being an actual house of worship was in 1839. The first church was built of coral rock. It was destroyed by a hurricane on October 11, 1846. The second church was rebuilt on the spot. The first service was on June 30, 1848. This is the church building you attended. Unfortunately, almost twenty years after you graced the doors, the church was destroyed by The Great Key West Fire of March 31, 1886. The modest wooden twenty-eight by sixty-six foot building was replaced by the next St. Paul's sanctuary, which was destroyed by a hurricane on October 11, 1909, the year before your passing. The last St. Pauls still stands today. It was built of concrete and opened it's doors on Palm Sunday Morning, June 8th, 1919. Twenty years ago, one million dollars worth of work and restoration was

54

performed on it. It is a truly magnificent church at the corner of Eaton and Duval Streets.

Sam, a stones throw away, one block to the east of St. Paul's, is the Key West United Methodist Church located at 600 Eaton Street. In 1994 I was baptized at the age of 39 in that grand house of worship after experiencing a harrowing event at sea that nearly claimed me. So harrowing was it that by escaping it, I had some thanks to give. The tide of epiphany swept me into the baptismal tankard like a ship being launched down the rails. Man, was I eternally thankful for not becoming shark-poop. In a later letter I will give the account of the Ides of March, 1994. To do so now would be a tangent. God knows, these messages are best attempted by not talking in circles. I think I feel you here time to time looking over my shoulder. I appreciate the help. I find comfort and some brethren-ship with you regarding the short distance between St. Pauls Episcopal and The Key West United Methodist Church. Both of us entered to give thanks for being released from a painful, long death at sea. Though I believe both of us waver in faith, I also believe there are no atheists in foxholes nor among stricken mariners. You gave your thanks on Eaton Street one hundred and forty seven years before I did. Nearly a century and a half later, I walked out of my church onto Eaton Street feeling as you did, gifted with another chance or opportunity approved by the Almighty, (however long that might last), and as freemen from Missouri tramping around a glorious piece of paradise ready for the next adventure, that hopefully won't kill us.

I have more to say about Key West, Sam. I have to go and take care of some business...run the dog and do a bit of research. I will get back to you in the next message. Thank you...

Hambone

Message Twelve...
"Key West"
January 19, 2014
Cape Girardeau,Mo

Dear Sam,

After church, you once again boarded the San Francisco and continued the voyage to New York, minus the twenty one passengers who refused to continue on aboard the cholera hosting ship. Personally speaking, I think those of you who did sail, had great courage and determination. Only a day and a half earlier you had finally landed and with great relief, you set foot ashore away from the smell of death and the vile scents and sights which led up to the free reign of mortality on the decks and in the cabins of the ship. In, **"Pudd'nhead Wilson's Calendar"**, you defined courage. You said..."*Courage is the resistance to fear, mastery of fear...not absence of fear. Except a creature be part coward, it is not a compliment to say he is brave; it is merely a loose misapplication of the word.*" You did feel terror as the San Francisco entered the Gulf Stream miles off of Key West. But, you had it mastered. You quaked, yet you stood and after the loss of two more passengers, you saw the skyline of New York on the morning of January twelfth, twenty eight passengers short of what you left the city of San Francisco with. Seven were dead, and twenty-one stayed who did not master fear. Without courage, they remained behind in Key West. Now, I wonder if any remained and have descendants in the Keys. I will have to look into that. I wonder things. Maybe too much...but I do wonder.

Although you are in New York, in a manner of speaking...I am staying behind in Key West for a bit. I want to tell you a few

57

things that I consider important for this bundle of spectral correspondence.

Many buildings still stand today that you saw in Key West. I have no clue of how many homes are included. If you walked past the icehouse doubling as a morgue at 428 Greene Street, I imagine you were pleased you were not a temporary occupant of this dwelling of the dead due to the tragedy on the San Francisco. The building has passed through time and purposes since it's construction in 1851. In the 1890's it was a wireless telegraphic station. During the Spanish American War in 1898, news of the sinking of The battleship, Maine, was released via its airwaves in order to inform the rest of the world. A cigar factory occupied the building in 1912. I know that brings you joy. You did have a taste for hand wrapped, Cuban, Key West Cigars as your letter from Key West affirms. Later on, the building was a bordello and several speakeasies.

Photo...Sam Milner

In the early thirties, Joe Russell opened "Sloppy Joe's Bar" and operated it until 1937. Other businesses came and went until 1958 when Captain Tony Tarracino opened, "Captain Tony's", a bar that's still open to this day. I have spent many afternoons in "Captain Tony's" quenching my thirst on humid, muggy and hot Key West afternoons while in port after expeditions to the Atocha site with fresh memories of found treasure and artifacts burned into my mind.

Over the years many notable personalities have quaffed their favorite elixir at "Captain Tony's". The barstools they used have their names painted on them. The famous names of John F. Kennedy, Harry Truman, Truman Capote, Duane Cahill, Jimmy Buffett, Shel Silversteen, John Prine, Mel Fisher and Ernest Hemingway...to name a few, have their reservations embossed by name on the spindly, plain stools. Ernest Hemingway is the main reason I've given you a quick history lesson about this hole in the wall bar on Greene Street. Hemingway won the Nobel Prize award for literature in 1954 for writing the novel, **"The Old Man And The Sea"**, and wet his whistle at "CaptainTony's" many times after writing in his studio on Whitehead Street. (By the way...1954 was the year of my birth.)

The great Hemingway spoke of your influence on American Literature. Your one and only peer in our literature had this to say about you. "All modern American literature comes from one book by Mark Twain called, **"Huckleberry Finn"**. It's the best book we've had. American writing comes from that. There was nothing before. There has been nothing as good since". Hemingway wrote this in his 1935 offering... **"The Green Hills of Africa"**. I have to wonder if Hemingway knew of your visit to Key West almost sixty years earlier and if he spouted this quote to his fellow drinkers in the confines of what is now, "Captain Tony's".

Hemingway had a home at 907 Whitehead Street, not far from "Captain Tony's". In his studio he wrote notable classics such as, **"Green Hills of Africa"**, **"To Have and to Have Not"**, **"The Snows of Kilimanjaro"**, and, **"The Happy Life of Francis**

Macomber". I do wonder if you strolled past the home which was built by local shipwreck salvor, Asa Tift, in 1851. In your letter from Key West you mentioned the Bahama Village area and the Key West Lighthouse. Both are very close to The Hemingway House.

Though your path with Hemingway crossed decades apart. You impacted him. You impacted us, doubly. You impacted us directly with your books, stories and letters. By impacting Hemingway, you impacted us again. Hemingway's stories and books about regular heroes struggling through adversity comes from the pages of, **"The Adventures of Huckleberry Finn"**. Ernest took the example and ran with it. He grew it. He cultivated it into some of the finest literature the world has ever known. Ernest was born in our "sister state" of Illinois, across the mighty Mississippi River. I like that. It makes perfect sense

Goodnight Sam. I will mail this soon. The river is too slow and low at the present. More from Key West in the next message. There is more. So much more. Thank you...

Hambone

Dear Sam,

Mel Fisher, as well as you, brought to light the insidious practice of slavery in America. Your writings, and Mel's artifacts, did their part to deliver the dark convention of human bondage into the minds of anyone who read them and to the hands who held them. In **"The Adventures of Huckleberry Finn"**, we follow Huck and Jim. While Jim is an escaping slave, so is Huck as he escapes physical confinement and beatings from his father. Time is too short to cover the whole story on these pages. I'm sure that you know it anyway. In your lecture notes you wrote..."A sound heart is a surer guide than an ill-trained conscious." When you spoke of the book you said..."A book of mine where a sound heart and a deformed conscious come into collision and conscious suffers defeat". The sound heart of Huck was able to over rule any notion that slavery was good or justifiable and it could not continue to be administered because it was the norm of the past and present. Huck's sound heart defeated his deformed conscious. How many sound hearts have been liberated from the enslavement of a deformed conscious after reading, **"The Adventures of Huckleberry Finn"**? The total number will never be known. I do know that anyone who read it, loved Huck. To love Huck includes approval of his gained acceptance and respect for Jim. Very few readers walked away without approving of every component of his good nature, charming ways, and his youthful self...conquering adversity and all dangers of the body and mind by defeating them and casting them away.

Mel's impact on the horror of slavery was in making it possible for us to actually touch the physical artifacts connected directly to the slave trade during the year 1700. In that year, an English slave trading ship, Henrietta Marie, sank twenty six miles west of Key West. You passed near her, "a-washed bones", on the choleric, San Francisco heading to Key West. While you would've been quite familiar with her lost cargo, we are taken aback in modern times when confronted with it's evidence. When Mel discovered the wreck of the slave ship, Henrietta Marie, the shackles for the children who were in bondage spoke of the horror cast upon the most innocent of the Africans. The Henrietta Marie was only sixty feet long, yet could

Edward Windsor Kemble drawing from first edition of... "The Adventures of Huckleberry Finn"

hold 200 souls in her cargo space. While the souls who drowned on the Atocha thought their plight could not be any worse, at least their hands were unshackled and their feet unchained, unlike the crammed humanity in the dark confines of the belly of other slave ships. When Mel discovered the Henrietta Marie in 1972, he was searching for the Atocha which would elude him for thirteen more years. After partially salvaging the ship and deciding it was not the "golden ship" he was pursuing, Mel moved on. Ten years later, Mel sent another expedition to further investigate the **Henrietta Marie**. This team unlocked the secret of what she really was. These days you might find the artifacts and the story of the **Henrietta Marie** making its way around the country. Some of those who line up and view her physical artifacts and history come with a sound heart. Some come out of curiosity with a deformed conscious. How many strong hearts defeated a deformed conscious after viewing the artifacts of slavery? There is no way of knowing. I do believe the battle against our sound hearts has been softened by the power of the words in, **"The Adventures of Huckleberry Finn"**, and by the discovery, recovery and the history of the English Slaver, **Henrietta Marie**.

On November 19, 1941 you were quoted by your sweet Clara in a letter to The New York Herald Tribune. "Our Civil War was a blot on our history, but not as great a blot as the buying and selling of Negro souls." Although you were born and raised in a slave state, personally witnessing the trafficking of slavery first hand, your sound heart was not corrupted by the deformed consciousness of the era. Thank you for delivering Huck to us. Your message is loud and clear for the ages.

More from Key West in the next message, Sam. Thank you for your help...

Hambone

Dear Sam,

     I haven't written for a week or so even though time to do so has been plentiful. We've been stuck inside mostly due to an unusually frigid winter. Outside activities have not been a factor. I've been stuck and my hindrance cannot be labeled as "writers block". It has more to do with once again asking myself... "What in the hell am I doing?" It's a tough task to write! While each message takes only a few minutes to read, a week to ten days is involved in the time it takes me to grind-out each one. Each short script takes close to eight hours total to complete. Tonight's victory will be achieved finishing this paragraph. I don't know how you did it, Sam. You wrote with great frequency in large quantities. Ink flowed through your veins to be released by your prolific hands. Yes, hands. In your later years you trained yourself to write left handed, giving relief to the rheumatism in the right. In even later years you dictated, as was the case of your autobiography which was published one hundred years after your exit with Halley's Comet in 1910.

     There are but a few people that I have shared these messages with. They, being confidants of mine, comes with a problem. They consist of; My Dear Debs..., My Sweet Sister Brenda..., and several close friends. I know they love and respect me as family and friend. Are these the critics I should enlist? I ask for criticism and counsel apart from our mutual affection and history.

Besides my lacking punctuation skills, misspelled words and sentence structure...they have praised the contents of the messages and have urged me to go on as if they, themselves... looked forward to the next one. Their approval of what they have read in the last few letters, along with their enthusiasm, has been enough to drive me back to my office in order to continue my communications to you.

I have a backlog of messages to seal in bottles and send on their way to you. The river, our river...has been low and choked with ice for going on a month now. The situation creates futile conditions for a message in a bottle. I need a good five knot current and at least a depth of twenty feet showing on the gauge in order to send your mail with efficiency. Without a strong current, they will travel a hundred feet or so and then wash up on the bank. Even though a short traveled message worked out great for young Dawson, I'd like for the messages to float at least past Cape Girardeau, Memphis, and beyond. It would be great if one was found farther south in the Gulf Of Mexico. The point being is...that I do write with some ease after I have launched a message. It is still difficult, yet easier. I will toss a few this weekend when I work on the Mississippi wreck. The temperature is forecast to be fifty degrees on Saturday and Sunday. If the river drops to seven feet as expected, the Amy Elizabeth will be fully exposed. I am curious to see how much overburden the river has stripped from her. During my last examination of the wreck three weeks ago, we made an incredible discovery in the muck. I will fill you in on that soon. I'll launch a message or two at the wreck-site.

In **"An Authors Soldiering"**, 1887, you said... "It is of no use to keep private information which you can't show off". I will go with that, Sam, although I sometimes feel the parallels should be kept to myself as a personal trove, yet... showing them off has been fun.

Goodnight, Sam. Its time to settle in and dream of summer...

Hambone

Dear Sam,

It's another cold day here at the Cape. This is the first time I've written you during the daytime. I'm used to a small lamp illuminating my keyboard and the glow of the computer screen as an assist. Today however, my room is brightly lit. I opened the blinds and flooded this space with light. I'm not sure I like the atmosphere. It may not be conducive to writing, but...I'll give it a try. There's something to be said for writing when darkness falls. For me, they go together. Our imagination flows better at night. The day consumes our thoughts and energy with matters of "have to's" and "want to's". Night is a time of unwinding and knowing that the demands of the day, yet unfinished, have been shelved until the next. The mind is allowed to flow without hindrance. Yep...I prefer to write at night.

I ended message thirteen with Key West as the unfinished subject. The parallels between you and Mel are strong on the island. The place you took a brief respite from the San Francisco after passing near the sunken treasure of the Atocha is where her tons of silver, gold and artifacts were brought ashore, and continue to be on display for almost thirty years now. While the discovery and recovery of the Atocha was a fantastic one, it is not a complete one. In 1985 we found her lower hull section of the galleon pinned down by over one thousand bread-loaf sized silver bars, ballast rock and several hundred pounds of gold and artifacts of every kind and type that were needed for the long voyage to Spain. What we did not find is the stern-castle of the ship. It was torn away from the hull along with the upper decking by a second hurricane in October, 1622. The stern-castle contained the rarest and most valuable items, which were under the guard of the Captain, Bernadino de Lugo, in his quarters. From the "X", where we found the main cultural deposit of the Atocha, (lower hull), in 1985, there is a trail of ship-parts, coins, pottery, artifacts and bones that extend into a corridor of twelve miles. As the stern-castle rafted upon the torn away upper-deck in the second hurricane, it lost treasure on the bottom for that great length. Someday the crews working the site will come across another King's ransom when they find the main bulk of the stern-castle of the Atocha. It will be a site to behold in the crystal clear blue water and could immediately double the value of the wreck by two fold. The Nuestra Señora de Atocha could become a billion dollar shipwreck!

Sam, you said..."There comes a time in every rightly constructed boy's life that he has a raging desire to go somewhere and dig for hidden treasure". Mel Fisher had the raging desire. His initial success was in finding priceless amounts of treasure from a doomed flotilla of Spanish Galleons that sank off the east coast of Florida in 1715. After his success there, he set his sights on the Atocha. You had a raging desire too, Sam. How much pirate gold did you seek on Jackson's Island in your youth...and when you remembered those boyhood expeditions that you put to paper your own self reliving those dreams of gold days as Tom Sawyer? I'd like to think that at least once, you said to Tom Blankenship…*"Today's the day we find treasure, Tom! Today's the day!"* It is plausible that you may have also yelled Mel's trademark battle-cry for treasure to be found!

Mel's raging desire to find another bonanza, the top treasure bonanza, came to fruition after a sixteen year search fraught with hardships of assorted kind. Operation costs for Mel's salvage boats and crews could run into thousands of dollars a day. During my time with Mel, I can vouch for this. Greedy State and Federal entities consumed the Fisher's time and scarce funds by attempting to seize Mel's discovered fortune, which was rightfully his, especially more so considering the loss Mel and Deo suffered because of the Northwind tragedy.

Mel found the treasure he raged for. The manifested treasure and the smuggled riches, such as raw Columbian emeralds, enriched Mel, his investors and his employees to a level that many had never been. Just as important, the Atocha was real! It truly existed. Mel wasn't crazy. He wasn't some kind of criminal fleecing people for money to invest in an outrageous quest and claims of a golden "ghost ship". Sadly, a huge price was paid by the Fishers. All of their newfound wealth could not buy back Dirk, Angel or Rick. A price was paid. No returns allowed.

Sam, you too found millions of dollars in treasure, and like Mel…you shared it with the world. I'm not speaking of your toiling in the dark dusty mines of the Comstock Silver lode in 1862. In 1863 you took the name, Mark Twain, while working for a newspaper in Virginia City, Nevada. Virginia City was built astride the silvery lode. Your golden treasures were the books you wrote, in particular, **"The Adventures of Tom Sawyer"**, (1876), where

Tom finds treasure. The effort to find it was fraught with danger, as was Mel's quest for the Atocha. While you had little success as a hunter of treasure in the form of silver ore in the mines of Nevada, you conjured-up the treasure you sought in the form of written gold. Tom dragged the treasure out of the cave and in a sense, handed it to you in the form of the vast riches you earned from all of your books. While, **"The Adventures of Tom Sawyer"**, was not a huge commercial success in the beginning, it was the purest of gold sparkling for all eternity as is the Atocha's. Tom was the catalyst for your wealth and fame to come. In 1885, one hundred years before Mel's 1985 discovery of the Atocha motherlode, you released, **"Adventures of Huckleberry Finn"**. The surprise twist of Tom entering the story and helping Huck free Jim from the Phelps family, cemented the bonds of Tom and Huck and propelled both writings into eternity. Tom, like Huck, demonstrated that he too, had won over any trace of a deformed conscious with the ammunition of a strong heart.

In message sixteen we will return to Hannibal. I've found many other items on the grounds of your home. Some are ordinary...some are fantabulous! That's a "Mel saying".
Goodnight......

Hambone

70

Dear Sam,

During my visits to your boyhood home in Hannibal last summer I found other interesting things under the grass besides the red lettered, **"D"-"A"-"Y"**, spelling painted on the three quarters. Some were mundane and unidentifiable while others were quite exciting. One useful artifact I found was an iron hook around three inches long. I unearthed it in the east courtyard where your second floor bedroom overlooks the yard. It was buried six inches under the grass and made my detector whine loudly. It appears to be a hanger for a lantern. This I cannot say one hundred percent. Until I find out otherwise, that's what I'm claiming it to be. I have no evidence that it belonged to your family and never will. It does, however, reach out to us from past dwellers of the property. Someone lost it there. Time, rain and gravity did their job. It is in good shape after decades, maybe even a century, in the wet and soft Missouri mud.

I have uncovered dozens of nails, bottle caps, aluminum, chunks of iron, wire and other modern scrap. Every time the detector beeps, indicating metal under the soil, it quickens my pulse. Whether the targets which I dig up are historic or scrap, it takes fifteen to twenty minutes to properly uncover, remove and mark the spot with measured triangulation and GPS. Also, I photograph them and take the time to repair any obvious damage to the fine lawn and sacred dirt that's been disturbed. When an artifact is buried deeper than most, it can take up even more precious time and effort. It is a slow methodical process, to say the least. One out-of-line swing of the detector can result in the passing-up and the non-recovery of a great find. I drive four hundred miles, round trip, when I go to Hannibal to search for artifacts. Twice, I have been to the home. So far, I've stayed two days on each trip. When I'm there, the time is too short but the memories are of a lifetime. It's interesting...looking, finding and trying to locate the treasures you left behind.

Your boyhood home on Hill Street was built in 1843. Your family moved in right away. After residing there for nine years, you left in 1854. In the years after the occupation by your family, it was used as a residence until 1911. The home was due to be demolished, however...the efforts of the Hannibal Commercial Club and its purchase by Mr. George A. Mahan saved it's eradication from history. Mr. Mahan fixed it up and gave it to the City of Hannibal in 1912. For 102 years it has been a museum visited by people from all around the globe. I would bet a citizen of every country has marveled at this historic house and has "aaahh'd" over the artifacts contained within. We are adding to the artifact collection, no matter how small, with every important piece I pluck from the work and play-yard of your youth.

Several other artifacts I've found on my dirt scratching sojourns to Hannibal are fantastic! During my second expedition I was detecting the vacant lot on the west side of your home. The ground was hard from being sunbaked in drought. It was a hot, gnatty day. My back was aching and my knees were sore from what seemed to be an endless series of holes that produced metal rubbish. The spa at my hotel was calling my name and my stomach was rumbling in anticipation of a dinner of fried chicken livers I'd promised it earlier. I decided to quit for the day. As I headed toward the gate, I swept the detector as I advanced. The detector beeped and indicated a strong signal at a depth of five inches. In my fatigued and hungry state I eyed the gate handle as a quick exit and considered examining the latest un-dug find in the morning fully expecting it to be nothing more than another nail, washer or another small chunk of featureless iron. I leaned my detector against the fence squatted next to it, lit a smoke and took a break. There was no way this Curious George was leaving with a hit un-dug. I opened a bottle of water, sat in the grass and daydreamed.

After taking a break, I got up, picked up the detector and swept it over the grass until I found the target. I centered my detector coil over it and pushed a small marker into the earth to establish the exact center of the hit. I laid my detector aside, got on my hands and knees, (groan, snap, crackle and pop), and examined the ground. Seeing nothing exposed on the surface, I used my pointed trowel to carefully remove a plug of dirt around the marker. I placed the plug a foot from the hole, got up and swept the detector over the plug and heard a strong signal. I examined the plug and discovered...another modern wire nail. It's always procedure to recheck a hole after recovering an item from it. On occasion, another artifact will share the same space. If a hole is not reexamined, there is a chance of not recovering another piece of history. I learned this lesson as a diver on the Atocha on Christmas Eve, 1985. I was detecting around the remains of her when I got a hit on my underwater detector. It turned out to be an iron barrel-hoop that held together one of the storage barrels of the galleon. A nice artifact yes. Gold or silver...

no! I laid the hoop aside and rescanned the hole. My headphones screamed of a huge mass of metal still buried deeper. I stuck my gloved hand into the muck of the seafloor up to my elbow and felt a smooth, elongated object. Digging like a dog, literally, for ten minutes made it possible to finally dislodge the artifact from the suction of the salty ooze. I lifted it out with great awkward effort and laid it next to the hole. I hand-fanned the cloud of mud away from it so I could see it. It was a fifty pound silver bar! I shouted with excitement into my regulator, marked the spot and tucked the treasure under my arm and headed to the surface. I returned to the hole later to recover the barrel hoop. In my euphoria, I had left it next to the hole. I rechecked the hole for more treasure. Nothing!

Native American scraping-tool

Sorry if I digressed, but a second sweep of the hole in your yard produced another hit. Sure enough, it was another nail. I did a third sweep after removing the second nail and the detector remained quiet. At least I had tried. As I began refilling the hole I noticed a rock in the bottom of the hole. Naturally my detector does not detect rock. I reached in the hole and with some effort, the rock popped free. Right away I knew the rock was actually very unique, historical and had to have been there during your time at the home! Sam...it was an Indian artifact! And it was a beaut. At first I thought it was a large arrowhead. I wiped away the remaining dirt clinging to it and it soon became evident that it was not an arrowhead. It looked more like a spearpoint. As I stood there pondering this totally unexpected find, I heard a voice ask me what I had found. I looked up and saw a workman who'd been working on power lines in the area. I showed it to him and he said his fellow lineman was an expert on Native American artifacts, and would be back from lunch in a few minutes. I immediately thought to myself, "What a timely coincidence." I asked the man to send his friend over to have a look and possibly identify it, if he could. He agreed to do so. What I saw on the artifact next was incredible, rare and truly unique.

I'll continue this story in the next message, Sam. We are having a major winter storm named, Titan, bearing down upon us. The wind is howling outside. Freezing rain, sleet and snow are kicking our butts. I heard a loud crash outside. I'd better go have a look. As long as the power remains on, we will be alright. Goodnight...

Hambone

Dear Sam,

We survived the big blow last night. In spite of ice, strong winds and snow...we kept electrical power. Your experience with electricity was in the beginning days of it's development and use. Your good friends Nicolai Tesla and Thomas Edison would be astounded beyond their wildest dreams of the impact their hell's spark has created. We are so dependent on it now, for civilization to go even a short time without it in these times is a matter of grave consequence.

Now...back to the Native American artifact I was contemplating in your yard on that sweltering Hannibal day. While I awaited the timely blessing of an actual expert to evaluate the artifact, I examined it closer. It had no notches at it's base for securing it to a shaft with sinew. It was symmetrical and finely worked along the edges. And, due to its sharpness, the implement was still capable of cutting flesh. The artifact measured three inches by 2 inches and was mostly white stone with some brown coloration. Under closer scrutiny, I noticed a fossil. My heart skipped a beat! Sam, imbedded in the artifact was a shell fossil! What type of shell I cannot say, nor can I say if it's a Mississippi River shell, or from the ancient ocean. Seconds after I noticed the fossil, the much touted expert walked up. After a greeting and a handshake, I gave him the artifact to examine. He immediately announced it to be an authentic scraper, a hand tool used for many tasks by Native Americans. It was used for scraping hides, as they were rendered for common use such as processing clothing, shelter and blankets. It was also a general cutting tool. For some reason, the expert hadn't noticed the fossil on it. I pointed it out and asked his opinion of it. After studying it closely, he told me it was very unique. It was the first example of a fossil on any Native American artifact that he'd seen in his passionate hobby of choice. After a bit, he went back to work on the power lines. I marveled at his grace shimmying up a pole to the mass of wires addling him.

I packed up my gear and trudged my way up Hill Street and back to my lodgings. Yes, the spa was healing, and the chicken livers were sublime! As I lay in bed satiated, clean and comfortable, I held the freshly scrubbed scraper and eyed it by the glowing light of the bedside table. With a chuckle and a bit of awe, I whispered..."I guess you left this behind, Injun Joe. I hope you don't come looking for it tonight," and turned off the light. After a bout of tossing and turning, I got up and checked the locks on the door. Then, I returned to bed and fell back into the sack. Injun Joe didn't invade my sleep as he did Tom's. I snored until first light.

The next morning I decided to nickname the scraper, Injun Joe. Finding the shell fossil in it reminded me of the thousands of shells of numerous specie, size, and color...that surrounded and were a part of the Atocha's remains. On occasion, what appeared to be a gold doubloon, turned out to be a round, golden shell. There was no mistaking silver pieces of eight. Their black, silver, sulphide coloration had an unmistakeable contrast on the sandy bottom. Most of us stuffed our pockets with the most prized shells while swimming along the seafloor with metal detectors in hand. Only the finest specimens made it to our net-meshed bags. The slightest chip or deformation triggered rejection. Our collections of these natural treasures of the sea were impressive. They made great gifts for our landlocked friends and wenches we wished to impress when we returned to the Port of Key West to make repair, spend our money and prepare our salvage boats for the next expedition. A pirate's life it was. The company personnel of "Treasure Salvors, Inc." worked hard...and...they played hard!

The scraper is a real treasure, Sam. Beyond the physical qualities I have described, it means much more than it's inherent self. Although I have found and kept a dozen items from your former home, the scraper is the only artifact that I can certify as having been present on the grounds during your youth. It fits the bill for this inquiry. It is the type of item I seek. I wonder how it arrived there. It could have been dropped by a Native American centuries ago. Perhaps it was buried for ceremony, a sort of offering to a hunting deity. All I know is...that you walked over it, Sam. It was there all the time, below the surface among the moles, worms and insects. It was a great experience finding it. Had he found it, young Sam Clemens would have felt as I did. I apologize for beating you to it Sam...one hundred and fifty years late.

In a letter to W. D. Howells dated February 22, 1877 you wrote, "Knowledge of Indians and humanity are seldom found in the same individual". I think this private message to Mr. Howells expressed your true feelings about the Native Americans. This contradicts the portrayal in many of your stories and books. Just as it did for slavery, your sound heart over-rode any deformed conscious you possessed. Slavery was a centuries old aberration when you spoke out against it in..."**The Adventures of Huckleberry Finn**". You couldn't do the same in a forum supporting the savage. The Native Americans were seen as an immediate danger, whether real...or imagined.

It's getting late. There are more finds to tell you about. I will continue in the next message. Goodnight, Sam...

Hambone

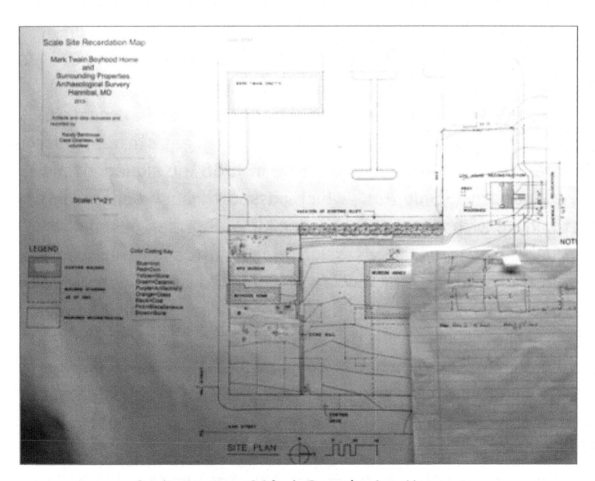

Scale site map of Mark Twain boyhood home.

Message Eighteen…
"Cape Wreck"
March, 8, 2014
Cape Girardeau, Mo.

Dear Sam,

A few weeks ago, I sent the 2013 site report of the sunken riverboat, **Amy Elizabeth**, to the Missouri Department of Natural Resources. The report covers all of the great new discoveries made about the wreck in the past year. I drew into the site-map the sections of the wreck that are newly visible. In the report, I made a case for the craft. I stated that it is unique and an important part of our local and state river heritage. The DNR is the agency that oversees and enforces regulations that apply when wrecks are being surveyed, investigated and excavated. Legally speaking, the wreck belongs to our great state of Missouri. Before President Reagan left office in 1988, he signed into law, "The Abandoned Ship Act", which passed through Congress at the last minute with the aid of Senator Lloyd Bentsen pushing it through. The law gave possession to the states, all shipwrecks within their waters. The law was a major blow to private wreck salvage-companies and individuals. As you can imagine, the layers of red tape, coupled with the politics of the, "Ivory Tower Archaeo-crats", have made it damn near impossible to get permission to actively dive on and recover history and treasure practically anywhere off the shores of our coastal states. I do have to say the Missouri Department of Natural Resources has been very cooperative with our work on the wreck, the **Amy Elizabeth**. Even though I can't excavate the hull to examine any contents it holds, as a non-certified archaeologist, the DNR has given me some latitude. Today, I received notification that my reports were excellent. I also detected some veiled excitement in the letter. I'm hoping it's a sign they're open to a greater degree

Exposed battery bank

of sending a team here to examine the bones of the **Amy Elizabeth**. That, would be great.

Since I told you about the wreck in messages seven and eight, another fantastic discovery was made last month. Erosion has revealed a bank of batteries in the stern area. Batteries are lined-up in a row beneath the gunnel of the port stern. There are probably more. The row of batteries disappear into the muck. Now, I see where all of the wiring that is visible leads to. To me, the amperage of the batteries would have been sufficient to start an engine and tells me without a doubt that the boat sank quickly and without intent. It was not scuttled as a boat deemed beyond usefulness. The batteries and items such as the cleat, steering mechanism and other parts would have been stripped from it first. I want to know what's in the hull. I need an archaeologist to step forward and dig. The river's done a fine job in the absence of a certified archaeologist. Sooner or later it will get to the point where the wear of the river on the overburdened shrouding of the boat will no longer be effective in revealing new detail. At that point, it will have to be excavated in a sound scientific manner by a credentialed archaeologist in order to unlock the mysteries held fast in the mud and rock that fills the hull.

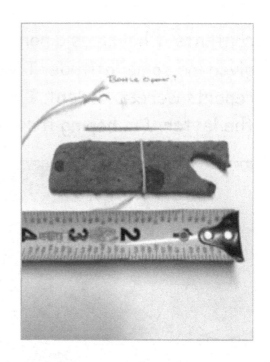

I realized when I signed-off in the last message, I said I'd reveal the other items I'd found in Hannibal last Summer. After receiving word from the Department of Natural Resources today, I admit the wreck became forefront of my attention, and...I wanted to share it with you. So, I guess we'll pick back up where I left off in the last message.

In the courtyard on the east side of the house, not far from the lantern hanger's resting place... I found a flat iron plate four inches by one inches long that appears to be a bottle-opener of some vintage. No markings nor date of manufacture unknown. In the vacant lot west of the home I found a spring hinge from a door.

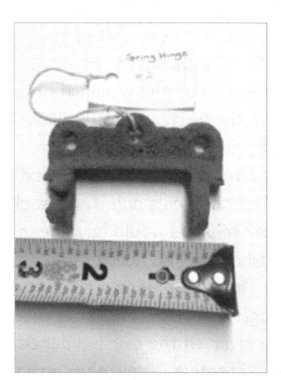

Also in the vacant lot west of the home, I found a steel disk measuring two and a half inches wide. No markings, date of manufacture unknown.
In what appears to be a dump-site on the northeast corner of the

property, I found several very unique items. I'm not sure of the beginning date of the site or why the items have never been disturbed. Perhaps it was washed out by rain before my first visit to Hannibal. It was then I first noticed mussel shells poking out of the ground. When I brushed one off and picked it up to examine it, I

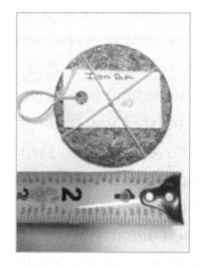

saw that it had five holes punched in it. I measured the holes. They were three quarter-inch in diameter. I knew that in the past, buttons had been made from shell. I assumed that this was a shell which had been used to make buttons. Some research in my room filled me in on the history of buttons made from mussel shells that were indigenous to the Mississippi River. From the late nineteenth

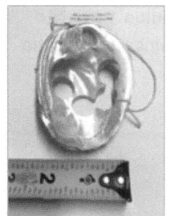

century to the early twentieth century, the manufacturing of buttons which were punched out of mussel shells was such a vast operation and with such great demand, the freshwater mussel population of the river flirted with extinction. The rise of plastics was a replacement for the tasty mussel and saved the species. Yes, the mussels did not die in vain as a fastener. As you know, they are also a tasty deep-fried treat. They are the clam of the inland waters. Finding the gouged-out shells reminded me of finding shells on the Atocha site, as did the fossilized shell on the native scraping tool. Am I seeing a theme here? Ha!

Sam, the next find was personal, yet it fit into all of the remarkable coincidences we have covered so far. In message eleven...I mentioned a catastrophe, without detail, that nearly claimed my life at sea on the Ides of March, 1994. Before I can enlighten you about the next artifact uncovered in your backyard, I have to tell you what happened to me on that fifteenth of March. I am finishing this message on the fourteenth. The Ides of March is upon us. As of tomorrow, twenty years have passed since the calamity I survived. The artifact is connected with the incident. It is a small world Mr. Clemens, but I wouldn't want to paint it. I will continue my Ides of March story tomorrow...on the Ides themselves. Goodnight.....

Hambone

Dear Sam,

On March fourteenth, 1994, Mike Fulmer and I were in "hog heaven". After six months of backbreaking labor and preparation, we were en route to the Atocha wreck-site to dive for sunken booty for a few days. The seas were calm and the weather was perfect. We had provisions to last a week. Our dive gear and metal detectors were in great repair and although our boat wasn't of great size, it was adequate for two people to live aboard in relative comfort and warmth. Our run to the Marquesas anchorage was to take four hours. The plan was to spend the night anchored off the Marquesas and dive on the fifteenth and sixteenth. At that point, if things were going well we would either stay another day or two or head back to our anchorage in the seaplane basin on the Gulf side of Key West.

As we made our way past the chain of islands that led to the Marquesas we were exhilarated. I hadn't dove on the Atocha's bones since 1989. I was back Sam, returning as the captain and operations manager for another salvage company. Mike was my first mate, pilot and best friend. When he wasn't bending my ear, I was taking-in the surroundings as I thought of the old days on the Atocha main pile. Pangs of some regret racked me.

In 1989, I left Mel's "Treasure Salvors Incorporated" and Key West to pursue a degree in archaeology. I had learned enough to know shipwreck salvage was being clamped-down-on with tougher regulations. If I wanted to increase my chances for success in the future, I needed to be credentialed. I landed back in Cape Girardeau to attend the required courses at my old Alma Mater, Southeast Missouri State University. For income, I managed a municipal olympic sized swimming pool and taught swimming arts for the Cape Public School System. I became the City Aquatic Director and held that position for a year before resigning and heading back to Florida to work for a new treasure salvage company. The archaeology degree remained unfinished. The expedition I'm telling you about was the first one for the new company. Getting to this point nearly broke the company and crew. With the determination and dedication of the crew, we were finally good to go on a small scale.

Sam, in order to tell you the story of the last artifact I was relaying to you at the end of message eighteen, I have to continue with this story. The artifact I uncovered in your yard nineteen years after this expedition in progress is connected with it. Hold onto your seat. The next day is the Ides of March. It's gonna' get ugly!

Mike and I made it to the Marquesas on the late afternoon of the fourteenth and anchored on the lee of the island. Sardines, crackers, and cheese made a simple tasty supper on that beautiful piece of ocean. The beer was ice cold, but a small ration of two bottles was abided by. Other than passing ships in the distance, we were isolated from civilization. In past years I'd spent many nights at this same anchorage. After the work was done on the Atocha site, we'd pull anchor and go there for it's protection from sudden squalls, waterspouts and wind. I felt at home again on the sea, after a five year respite. Mike and I sat on the bow of the

86

boat and bull-shitted well into the night. It was one of those nights where the conditions were such, that the glow of the lights of Havana could be seen over the horizon ninety miles southward. The sea was calm and stars reflected off of the flat brine. It was our raft Sam. Treasure could be on deck the next day! Life was good. No one knew where we were. That.....was our first mistake!

Sam...in, **"The Refuge of the Derelicts"**, you wrote..."There are no accidents, all things have a deep and calculated purpose; sometimes the methods employed by Providence seem strange and incongruous, but we have only to be patient and wait for the result: then we recognize that no others would have answered the purpose, and we are rebuked and humbled." **If I may add to that quote, most accidents occur not as a result on one particular act, but in the culmination of a chain of smaller events that are not considered. The peril they prepare is not evident until the chain is long enough to lash you, leaving you little time to avoid injury or death, if you are skilled and lucky.**

I woke up on my bunk the morning of the fifteenth to the sound of Mike making coffee on the coleman stove. I feigned further sleep and smiled in anticipation of a thick cup of his Bustello Cuban Coffee, heavy with sugar and cream. What a great mate. He knew my habits well. After a cup or two of his caffeinated rocket fuel and a light breakfast, I'd be ready for the challenges of the day and diving. Few pleasantries were passed between us as we stared at the horizon and drank our swill. The weather and conditions were holding. In the distance the ocean was blue and beckoning. Gold fever swept over us. "Today's the day!" I said looking over at Mike. "It's a good day to dive!" I was making a joke....quoting Sioux leader, Crazy Horse's famous quote, "It's a good day to die." (H'oka-h'ey). Little did I know in the coming hours, that utterance would haunt me and make me aghast of it's prophetic imminence as I struggled to live.

After some cereal, juice and energy bars for breakfast, we prepped the boat for the three mile run to the Atocha site. We lowered the canvas roof, topped off the fuel tank with gas from the spare cans and warmed up the engine. It purred like a kitten. I climbed up on the bow as Mike pushed the boat forward. I pulled in the anchor-line and brought the anchor aboard. Then, I turned to Mike and gave the thumbs up. He pulled back on the throttle and within a few moments we were up on a full plane. I stayed on the bow and watched for any hazards we might encounter as we sped along. We had no dolphin to escort or join us for a ride on the bow wave, but a few flying-fish scampered about slapping their tails on the water to gain speed for flight.

I worked my way back to the cabin holding tightly to the handrails and joined Mike in the cabin. As Mike's eyes glanced to the horizon and then back to the instruments, there was little said. Conversation wasn't necessary. The conditions were extraordinary and the excitement was palpable.

I will continue this in the next message, Sam. I gotta' go...

Hambone

Dear Sam,

This is a first…a two message day! I had things to tend to and went swimming at an indoor pool. I taught a swimming lesson while I was there.

Back to the telling of the events on the Ides of March, 1994. Mike and I arrived at the GPS numbers we had been heading to. When we found them, we circled the location slowly in the boat. Conditions on the site were as good as they get in March. Actually, they were exceptional. I picked up a marker buoy tied to a weight and coiled the line in my hand. I stood ready on the rail and waited for Mike's command to drop it overboard as we passed over the GPS location we'd picked out to dive on. He gave me the word and I dropped the buoy and line overboard making sure the line didn't foul the propellor. I told Mike we were all clear. He turned the boat into the wind and motored away from the buoy as I clambered back up to the bow and prepared the anchor for heaving. Seventy-five feet from the buoy Mike stopped the forward motion of the Bayliner and proceeded in reverse toward the buoy as I threw the anchor in, set it, and payed-out line as we backed down toward the buoy marking the first diving-site of the day. We set up nearly perfect in relation to the buoy. It tapped the bottom of our transom damn near dead center. He turned off the engine and we stood on the rear deck admiring our work, the scenery, and the anticipation of going overboard to scan the bottom for lost loot and artifacts of the **Nuestra Senora de Atocha,** the prize of the ill-fated fleet of 1622. Hambone was back in town!

After a couple juices and smokes we prepped for the dive. Knowing the currents in the area can become swift quickly, I attached extra line to our safety line. A safety line is a long length of line attached to a ring buoy. The line is attached to the boat and floated behind the boat. It is a safety device. If a diver is swept away from a boat due to current or exhaustion, the line can be grabbed onto. A diver can then work their way back to the boat, hand over hand, or be pulled in by the crew. With the addition of an extra twenty five feet that I added, the safety line was now around seventy-five feet. That would be plenty.....**second mistake!**

There was a slight current running already. Our plan was to work under the boat and proceed into the current. As seasoned divers, we followed this standard procedure. By doing so, one can use the current to swim lazily back to the boat. Diving with the current tends to sweep you too far from the boat and you have to fight the current in order to get back to the boat...in a usually tired or exhausted state. We put on our dive gear, checked each other out and with metal detectors and digging tools in hand, we jumped overboard, meeting at the transom next to the buoy that hopefully marked our glory hole. Our plan was to head into the current on the bottom and swim to the anchor to make sure it was securely fastened to the sea floor. We had to make sure the boat wasn't going to break free and drift away since there was no one on board to monitor calamities such as that.....**third mistake!**

The current had been building even more since our arrival, but the dive was still do-able. Our first dive was going to be a short one. After securing the anchor, we were going to metal-detect and do visual surveys between the anchor and the boat. Then, we were going to surface and make another dive plan, or... get out, rest and have a juice. I submerged first and dove to the bottom. There was a lot of sand on the bottom which makes for a poor handhold if one has to crawl along the bottom against a strong current. I noted that fact and waited for Mike. As I waited, I visually surveyed the bottom for obvious treasure or artifacts poking up through the swirling sand. I looked up and saw Mike coming down toward me. He descended about half way to my depth, stopped and headed back to the surface in what appeared to be a controlled calm manner. I figured he'd forgotten something or was having problems with his gear, or might be having inner-ear equalizing difficulty. I decided to give him a minute and returned my attention to my surroundings.....fourth mistake!

A couple of minutes passed before I surfaced to see what the holdup was. After the water drained from the faceplate on my mask, I looked around and didn't see Mike. I held onto the dive ladder, looked up and yelled for him but there was no reply from the boat. Next, I checked behind the boat. That's when I saw a mass of bubbles just below the surface that didn't look right. The bubbles of a diver in distress are easily recognizable. It appeared he had blown a high pressure hose because of the mass of swirling bubbles exploding to the surface. I quickly swam to the center of the calamity and dove straight down. Several feet under, I found Mike struggling. His regulator had dislodged. It was free flowing behind him and out of his reach. I faced him, put his regulator in his mouth and we slowly surfaced together. When we broke the surface I saw blood on his right ear. He was somewhat out of it and kept slipping beneath the surface. I reached out and filled his Buoyancy Compensator Vest with air to keep him on the surface with me. He regained cognition. I told him we had to return to the boat immediately. Just as I said that, I noticed something white float by my head. It was the ring buoy at the end of the safety line! During our struggle, the current had carried us along enough to put us in peril. If we could not swim against the current to the boat, we were in big trouble!

The current didn't seem very strong. Mike said he was okay and the bleeding had stopped. He had ruptured an eardrum. The cool salty water had entered the perforation of his tympanic membrane and caused nausea and vertigo. Even a skilled diver like Mike can and did become disoriented and nauseous enough to be put in peril by the symptoms.

Against the building current, we made a swim for the boat. By then, the ring buoy on the safety line was fifty feet from us. Side by side we kicked hard with our fins. Every ten seconds or so I raised my head to judge our progress and take bearings on the boat. After five minutes of kicking as hard as I could, it became evident we weren't making any progress. In fact, we were slipping backwards! I left Mike on the surface and dove to the bottom hoping to find a way to pull myself across the bottom to the boat. On the bottom I forced my hand deep into the sand in order to get leverage enough to pull myself along. Each effort only gained me inches of travel. The sand was too fine to work with and my air supply was half used up. In order to get back to the boat we were going to have to go-for-it on the surface. I ascended to rejoin Mike, I realized I was around forty feet behind him. My round trip to the bottom had cost me more distance from the boat!

Without communication, Mike and I knew we had to somehow get back to the vessel on our own or die of exposure or shark attack in Straights of Florida. We were being swept out to sea in the direction of Cuba. No one knew where we were. We were on our own. I put my head down, and kicked with all my might. After a while, I looked up. I was farther from the boat! In spite of my effort, I was still sliding backwards to doom. I laid my head back, dug deep, kicked, and kicked and kicked. No progress! Only backsliding. The boat was becoming smaller. I was nearly 100 yards from it now. I had to keep tabs on it's location. Our last hope would be in our ability to find it when the tide slacked. That would be hours. My job now wasn't to get the boat, but to lessen my drift. At this time I couldn't even get a visual on Mike. Every time I stopped to yell his name, the current carried me further away. My hope was, that he'd made his way back aboard the boat and was prepping to come rescue me. Nearing exhaustion and an hour later, no Mike and no boat! I was alone. I laid my head back in the water and kicked...

One hour passed.....and then another one. I had drifted farther from the boat despite the effort I was exerting. Cramps racked every muscle in my legs and feet but there was no stopping to rest. Even a minute's pause to rest would cost me distance. Every so often I'd stop and yell for Mike...but...got no reply. It crossed my mind Mike may be already gone. I felt very alone and saddened when I considered the worst case scenario. If the tide didn't slack soon, there was no way I could continue attempting to get back to the boat. I would run out of energy and let go with the rushing current. I knew I had a whistle for summoning any rescuers within earshot. I didn't have a flashlight for signaling. Sunset was three hours away. We left no lights burning on the boat...**Fifth mistake!**

Above this fast moving tragedy, Comet Shoemaker-Levy 9 was heading to it's spiral of death. It will disintegrate when it hits Jupiter during the time frame of July 16-22, overlapping the discovery date of the Atocha nine years before on July 20. Caesar's end was entwined with a comet in 44 B.C. His Ides, and my Ides, were turning out to be very bad for the both of us, and for my best mate Mike. More Later...

Hambone

Dear Sam,

I just returned from the river. While I was there I mailed three more messages to you. I had a backlog of letter stuffed bottles to send. The current is swift enough again to carry them a good distance. The bottles sped downriver faster than any I have thrown so far. After they disappeared into the brown water and floating debris of branches and good sized trees, I sat on a bench surveyed the scene and contemplated finishing the story about Mike and me I'd left yet unfinished. Here it goes.......

As I kicked against the current another hour, it gave no sign it was going to end soon. Further attempts at summoning Mike were to no avail. Short blasts from my whistle weren't returned. Deeper concern for Mike's fate troubled me as I struggled against the mighty strength of the current. This can't be! Is this it? The joke I made earlier, "It's a good day to dive," occurred to me. What was I thinking? I frowned and continued swimming.

Mike was the first friend I made in Key West when I moved there in the Spring of '85. He was a lifeguard at a luxury resort where I too, was hired as a lifeguard. We had a lot in common. We laughed a lot, were both veterans of the army and had a love for the sea and the adventures it brings. In the eight years since our meeting, and the life or death situation we were in...we had become as close as brothers. As I thought about Mike and the times we'd gone through, I simply **could not** accept the fact that we were done. Reality told me otherwise as the cramping in my legs

95

and hips grew worse. For relief, I rolled over on my back to push against the water with a different angle of my fins. On my back I could see the blue sky. The reason it was so blue was due my heightened adrenaline-fueled senses. The sun was at about a thirty degree angle with the horizon. I estimated it would set within two hours as I kicked on my back and drew in the pure air. We'd been in the water struggling for over four hours.

As I laid on my back and kicked, I decided to roll back over on my stomach and go for it. The boat was still in sight but time was running out. Earlier, I'd ditched my scuba tank and metal detector in order to streamline myself. Sam, fate hangs in the balance by chance. Little did I know that my next move increased my chance of survival manyfold. Before I rolled over I prayed for help for me and my stricken companion. I rolled over to the right. An instant before my face plunged in...I saw a flash of white in front of me, and to the left. I had an idea what it was, and if it was what I thought...I had a chance. Mike and me had a chance.

Immediately, I treaded water to get a look at the white object bobbing on the waves. It was what I thought it was...a lobster trap buoy! It was stationary in the current. I knew it had a line attached to it and the line was attached to a heavy lobster trap on the seafloor. If I could manage to get to it, it would be an excellent handhold to grab onto to bring a halt to my suffering and widening distance from the boat. Had I rolled to my left to begin a final assault on the boat, I wouldn't have seen it. I roll to my right almost every time because I'm right handed.

I wasn't out of the woods yet. I still had to get to the buoy. It was upstream by at least fifty feet. I put my head down in the water and kicked for all I was worth. I raised my head to get my bearings every minute or so and saw I was gaining inches. Another half hour passed. I'd decreased the distance between me and the lobster trap by half. An hour passed. I was only a few maddening feet from it. Finally, at the end of my endurance..the buoy was inches from my fingertips. The last few centimeters of a gap between my fingers and my styrofoam salvation might as well have been measured in yards. Finally, my gloved fingertips touched it and it bounced away. I tried again and gained a hold with my extended right hand. I reached under it and seized the line it was attached to. I brought my left hand forward to double my grip. I slowly quit kicking to lessen the sudden introduction of my weight to the thin line. I was concerned that the line would snap or come loose from the trap it was tethered to. My other fear was the lobster pot dragging across the bottom as the current swept me. I stopped kicking, relaxed my tortured muscles and hoped for the best. The line did not part. The trap did not drag. I held onto the line. The first stage of my five hour ordeal was over. Then I thought of Mike.

It had been hours since I saw him last. I raised my head, spit out my snorkel and bellowed out his name. Nothing. I repeated and blew my whistle too. Nothing. A deeper reality crept in again. Was he still alive? Is he miles from me drifting as a speck on the ocean? I yelled and blasted my whistle and listened. Dusk was approaching soon. The sun was kissing the ocean. When I finally heard Mike's voice returning my last call to him, it was a prayer answered! He was alive and sounded fine. His distance from me was great enough that I couldn't see him. I didn't have to. I asked him what he was doing. He told me he was in the middle of a field of lobster buoys and was advancing toward me one by one! I told him I was clutching one and I would wait for him until he got to my position nearer to the boat. Mike arrived at my location. As he swam the distance from his last buoy to me, I extended my arm, grabbed his wrist and put the buoy line in his hand. Thankfully, the line held under the added weight.

Captain Mike Fulmer and Hambone, 2006. Photo: Christopher Fulmer

After a brief exchange of backslaps and conversation we decided to hang tight at our location and wait for the current to lessen. It was dusk. We changed our mind soon afterward when a chill came over me...the beginnings of hypothermia. Also, it was getting dark. Sharks would be roaming soon and feeding all night. I knew first hand the numbers of them that would soon arrive. We used to shark fish from the salvage boats at night while on the site in the eighties. A baited hook was a guarantee of catching and pulling one aboard. Then, we'd take pictures of them and toss them back where they belonged. One night we smeared spaghetti sauce on the mouth and face of a six foot tiger shark and posed as if it had bitten us. Pirate entertainment, I reckon.

On the count of three we let go of the safety of the buoy and kicked hard toward the boat. I knew immediately that I wasn't making progress. It was almost dark and all I represented at that point was a struggling warm body on the surface to any sharks present. I was making zero progress and the buoy was out of reach. I looked up at Mike. He was making progress, **real** progress, **unnatural** progress toward the boat. Every time I looked up, he was closer to the boat. It was as if an unseen hand was pulling him. Though I exerted all the effort I could muster in my now rested and un-cramped legs, I simply could not move forward. When Mike was within twenty feet of the boat, I treaded water and cheered him on with encouragement whether he heard me or not. To my amazement and relief, I saw him climb the dive ladder and board the boat. Seconds later I heard the engine start and watched him exit the cabin and move forward to the bow to pull the anchor. At that moment...I let go and drifted. I was spent and my mate was on the way to pluck me out of the drink. As Mike pulled the boat next to me, I felt reborn as I scaled the dive ladder. I fell over the gunnel onto the back deck. As Mike stood there looking at me, he said... "There ain't no way we were gonna' die on my Dad's birthday!" I had no

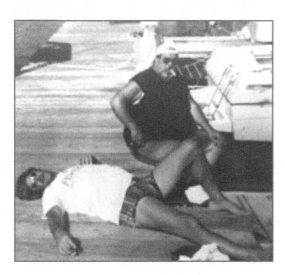

My brother, Don Barnhouse and Captain Michael L. Fulmer 1715 Fleet, 2004

idea that it was his Dad's birthday... that March the fifteenth. I'm glad it was! We took advantage of the remaining twilight to hightail it back to the Marquesas for the night. After we anchored and squared away the boat and gear...we chowed, had a few grogs, smoked ceegars and talked well into the night of our experience and how the hell it happened. Our pride was injured, our dive gear and detectors were lost, but...we were alive to tell the tale. Money can't buy that, but it can buy equipment.

Mike passed away three years ago unexpectedly. I miss my friend...my best mate. I have no doubt Mike would be searching with me in Hannibal if he was still around. Maybe he is....

Sam, to tell you about an artifact I found in your yard, I had to tell you about Mike first. On my last trip to Hannibal in 2013, I was running out of time on the final day as the sun was setting. Although I'd found some interesting items, I wanted to score a big prize before I left. Knowing I had time for digging only a few more holes, I decided to go with my gut and randomly pick a spot that felt **right**. I exited my grid area and wandered the property. I scanned a spot at the base of the stone wall that was built by the

WPA in the thirties to serve as a firebreak between your home and a long gone lumber mill. My detector beeped loudly, indicating a large hit under the dirt. I dropped to my knee and probed gently for the target with a long screwdriver. I touched something solid and metallic. With my trowel I  carved a divot and pulled it out. I looked in the hole. To my amazement I saw a plaque with writing stamped on it! It was badge shaped and around six by five inches. The inscription read, "**The Stewart Iron Works Covington, Kentucky.**" I was stunned. Mike was from Covington! I sat back in the grass, lit a smoke and reflected. Finally I whispered, "You **are** with me on this one too, my friend. That's how it outta' be." I loaded my van and drove back to Cape. My gut feeling had panned-out in a huge personal way. Goodnight... Hambone

Dear Sam,

In a letter to Mary Mason Fairbanks you wrote... "When we think of friends, and call their faces out of the shadows, and their voices out of the echoes that faint along the corridors of memory, and do it without knowing why save that we love to do it, we content ourselves that friendship is a reality, and not a fancy...that is builded upon a rock, and not upon the sands that dissolve away with the ebbing tides and carry their monuments with them."

In Notebook, 1898 you lent us this definition of friendship. "The proper office of a friend is to side with you when you are in the wrong . Nearly anybody will side with you when you are in the right."

What is it, Sam, that causes a friend to strike our fancy, usually immediately? Almost instantly we know that we want to be around this person. They add to the completion of yourself and the immediate scenario or task at hand, whether it be work or play. The platonic love and care for a friend elevates them to family status and sometimes, beyond description. Is it a selfish attraction? Do we see ourselves in them causing us to accept and elevate them? I'm sure it goes deeper, and besides...what do I know? I do know Mike was my brother and he was beyond a friend. Our relationship was symbiotic. He was my Huck. Mike is gone, yet he lives on in my memories.

Sam, when you left Hannibal in 1853 at the age of seventeen to work as an intern printer in St. Louis, you found a friend. It could be argued, one of your best lifelong friends...Jacob H.

Burrough. Fellow journeymen you were...he in chair-making and you in printing. Your paths crossed at the Pavey Boarding Home in St. Louis where you took up residence. Jacob, or Jake...as you knew him, was a voracious reader of many disciplines and had a keen sense of literary judgement. I see the attraction that bonded you and Jake as friends for life. Though he was ten years your elder, he saw something in a young man from Hannibal to give you notice of camaraderie, despite being an elder. I reckon Jake did have keen literary judgement. He read you like a book. I have to wonder what fragments, snippets and stories Jake was witness to during those St. Louie years by kerosene light at the home late into the night. What stories did he hear first hand from your personal experiences that were later cut, molded and shaped to fit the purpose of creating the worlds best literature? We can only speculate whether he encouraged you to embed wit, musings and anecdotal experiences to paper, or...whether his prompting was subtle or flat-out insistence that you grind over paper, pencil and ink sharing your otherworldly talent with us.

We all know when Jacob and you parted, your path led to the most revered position you'd always sought to attain, that of riverboat pilot. The "Big Muddy" led you to Captain Horace Bixby. Under his heel as a young apprentice pilot...every twist, oxbow and shoal of the Mississippi were committed to your memory. It was Bixby's way, or the waterway! Your life as, "one of the most unfettered men on the planet", came to an end with the outbreak of the Civil War. If I figure right, you piloted close to four years. What must have been a huge disappointment for you at that time, turned out for the best...the best for all of us. Had you not left the river, would you have been as prolific a writer? I can't imagine you wouldn't have written to a scale greater than many. Would we have a Mark Twain? Would the, "Lincoln of American Literature", be Hemingway instead of you? Would Hemingway have shined on his own without a Twain? Out of your short tenure behind the mast on the "Father of Waters" came your characters and stories in your writing. **"Life on the Mississippi",** alone would have given you spectacular notoriety.

I recently found out in the meantime, Jake moved to Cape Girardeau! The historical record places him here as a barrister and Union Captain serving as the Provost Marshal for this area during the Civil War. A few years earlier, around 1860, Jake moved from Spanish Street to the west, down Bloomfield Road, into a splendid brick mansion atop a hill overlooking the city and the dozens of acres that surrounded that great house. The

Burrough Mansion still stands today. It is in a great state of repair and maintenance. It serves as an office building for scores of apartments surrounding it on the former acreage, Jake tilled and labored on. Well...labor comes into question. How many lawyers do we see with dirty hands except in the figurative sense? Imagine my surprise, Sam... when my studying of your friendship with Jake led me to handwritten letters to him from you. The correspondences are on deposit at Southeast Missouri State University.

Burrough Mansion

Side view of Burrough Mansion

The pencil scrawled messages are in fine shape and reveal even more of your fond and deep friendship with him. The surviving letters were written on February 1868, June 1874, August 31, 1876 and November 1, 1876. Another letter survives in the University's archives written to you by Jake's son...Frank. It is dated December 20, 1900. Frank E. Burrough was a prominent attorney like his father. He served as the sixth prosecuting attorney of Cape Girardeau from 1891-1892. The letter, as you recall, was Frank's reply to a correspondence from you in which you reminisced about Jake to Frank. You wrote... "He and I were comrades & close friends.".

How fitting it is the letters between you and Jacob rest at the University? Jake was a member of the first board of regents at the institution. His vote was crucial in the decision, by a vote of 4-3, to locate the campus in Cape Girardeau. Cape was selected over Arcadia, Missouri as the city in which to locate the Normal School, present day Southeast Missouri State University. Your description of the school in, **"Life on the Mississippi"**, paid homage to our city, and specifically...the building your old friend had a major hand in locating at Cape Girardeau.

The fact you thought of your old friend so late in your life, well after the accolades of world fame enveloped you, speaks volumes of the friendship. A journal entry in your notebook... number twenty, page 456, places you in Cape Girardeau between April-May 1882, looking up and visiting Jake. As you put it..."Cape Girardeau & see Burroughs under secrecy." Your fame at the time was tremendous across and around the globe yet you sought out your old friend incognito from a prying world.

What a tribute to Jake you made when you used him as a character in, **"The American Claimant"**. The book was released in 1892, nine years after Jake's passing. Jake's character was a journeyman chair-maker and boarding house friend of the character, Howard Tracy.

I was thrilled to find out without a doubt, that your roommate and friend...Jacob H. Burrough, moved here. What I did not expect to discover was the strength of your bonds of friendship and what would materialize as I researched. Another letter has surfaced that reveals an amazing connection between you and our, "Sister City", Jackson, Missouri. I will leave that to another message, Sam. I need to get back to processing the latest artifacts I've recovered from the soil of your boyhood home in Hannibal during my October effort...

Hambone

Message Twenty-three...
"Best of Friends"
June 3, 2014
Cape Girardeau, Mo.

Dear Sam,

It's been a while since I've written. Swimming season has arrived with the passing of Memorial Day, which means retirement is over for me for the next six months. I have a swimming pool business. My time for the past month has been devoted to opening pools, servicing pools and recovering from the gauntlet of exhaustion, heat and a myriad of solutions for getting some infernal human aquariums up and running. I will be sixty this August 3rd, Sam. Labor isn't getting any easier. My smoking habit is not helping either. Neither did yours for you. Aaah hell, what's age anyway? What's important is not how old we are, but how old we feel. I don't feel nearly sixty, Sam. I feel nearly eighty. Hah!

Three weeks ago I gave a lecture at the Cape Girardeau River Heritage Museum. The subjects of the talk were Jake Burrough and you. My thesis was, you and Jake were not merely friends, but you were best friends. My argument was well received by the audience of twenty. There's some excitement at the Cape with the news that Samuel L. Clemens' best friend lived here in our fine city, and...the two of you corresponded after the St. Louis years and you slipped into town incognito to visit Jake at the Burrough Farm.

There are other candidates that stand out possibly as who you considered your best friend in life, besides your sweet Olivia, of course. One was the enigmatic and electromagnetic, Nikola Tesla. Your fondness for gadgetry and inventions, especially on the scale of Tesla's creations, drew you to him like a magnet, if you'll excuse the pun. To have been a fly on the wall during your times spent with him in the sulfury smelling "hell's kitchen" of his lab would have made for some remarkable eavesdropping. The conversations and antics of you two would have been like a real life Dr. Frankenstein meets Tom Sawyer, if I may be so bold.

The American realist author, playwright and literary critic... William Dean Howells, was also a great friend. William was considered, "The Dean of American Letters." Some have written, the Mark Twain we all know and cherish would not have been if not for the friendship and partnership between you and Howells. The greatest comparison I can make in our times are the musicians and songwriters, John Lennon and Paul McCartney. Without the meeting of these two "Liverpoolians", would there have been a Beatles? And without the Beatles, what would civilization be like today? The "fab four" certainly changed Western civilization, and the world, just as you and William transformed American Literature.

Joseph H. Twichell was also a close friend. He was probably in your closest friend category longer than anyone else including. Jacob Burrough, Nikola Tesla and William Dean Howells. Besides Tesla, I see a common thread presenting itself in the persons of Jacob, William and Joseph. All three of them were men of letters, literary critics and authors of a sizable number of books. Twichell was your best friend for forty years. He had the longest tenure as the one outsider you sought counsel from, a best friend. All of these best of friendships began with Burrough in 1853. The remaining three, Tesla, Howells and Twichell came later, yet all of the friendships overlapped until you passed.

Best friendship, or the deciding of whom our best friend in life will forever be, is an elusive pondering to me, Sam. As we look back to the past and consider the present, we have collected many greatest of friends. They seem to fit the time or phases of our lives as confidants who fill that role at a given time. We cross paths with them for some reason and decide we like them. Out of that platonic event fast-tracks a sort of kindred spirituality compelling us to be there for that person and to support whatever is going on with them, whether it be work, sport, play or disaster. We laugh the most with them, possibly to the chagrin of our wives on occasion. We dream with them, argue with them, and drop any foolish notions of what we consider ourselves to be and remain ourselves with our best friends. Think back, Sam. Decide who your best friend was and let me know. I don't think you can and neither can I. Like you, I've had four best friends, (imagine that). I can't say which of the best friends was the best one. Picking your favorite dog is the same dilemma. Once you've chosen the truest of the furry companion that pleased you most, it gets knocked back into the den of contestants and another rises to the top of favoritism, which lasts for only a shot while. We can't decide who our, "man's best friend", was or our best friend. That wouldn't feel right. And, if one say's they've achieved it, I will doubt them.

I'm pleased I discovered your friendship with Cape Girardeau resident, Jacob H. Burrough. Had I not started this bundle of letters to you, we wouldn't know the details of your Cape Girardeau connection. At the Southeast Missouri State University Library, the letters between you and Jacob are on deposit. It was a remarkable afternoon one day last month when I was able to examine the pencil-written correspondences between you and

Jake. To hold and examine what you wrote to your old friend was a great experience.

I'm going back for another look-see. I'm certain it will be as thrilling as the first time. It certainly seems full circle and satisfying the letters are being taken care of by the University and that Jake was so much a part of it's roots. I have to wonder if your quote in, **"Life On the Mississippi"**, concerning the odd looking towers of the school, was a tribute to Jake. I'm sure I will have to remain in wonder. Goodnight Sam...

Hambone

Dear Sam,

Not much has changed since I last wrote. My time has been filled with swimming pool services, domestic chores and responsibilities of every sort. I've been tired and lazy in the evenings, Sam. That's one of the reasons I haven't corresponded for over a month. I still have plenty more to write about, that's not the problem. During this hiatus I've been reading several of your works and planning this letter's content in my mind. We're going back to Key West in this message, Sam. Cayo Hueso, Treasure Island and the Magic Isle she has been labeled. Each brand fits. I'm kinda' partial to Treasure Island as a nickname for it, but The Magic Isle is a photo finish second place for the "Conch Republic" of Key West, Monroe County, Florida.

In, "**Adventures of Huckleberry Finn**", Huck describes the raft... "Sometimes we'd have that whole river all to ourselves for the longest time. Yonder was the banks and the islands, across the water **and** maybe a spark-which was a candle in a cabin window; and sometimes on the water you could see a spark or two...on a raft or a scow, you know; and maybe you could hear a fiddle or a song coming over from one of them crafts. It's lovely to live on a raft. We had the sky up there, all speckled with stars, and we used to lay on our backs and look up at them, and discuss about whether they were made or just happened. Jim he allowed that they was made, but I allowed they happened; I judged it would have took too long to make so many. Jim said the moon coulda' a laid them; well, that looked kind of reasonable, so I didn't say nothing against it, because I've seen a frog lay most as many, so of course it could be done. We used to watch the stars that fell, too, and see them streak down. Jim allowed they'd got spoiled and was hove out of the nest."

Denny Wayne

Sam, when I moved to Key West, I arrived pulling a camping trailer that contained all my possessions I'd held onto when I sold my home in Missouri and auctioned off its contents. I lived in said mobile lodging at a campground in "Old Town", Key West. I had it in mind to live in the camper until I found a proper houseboat to call home. It took only a few weeks of searching before I found the right boat. It turned out to be the perfect boat.

The houseboat, Denny Wayne, was not only my floating digs for almost four years, he was also my raft, Sam. He was my raft in many ways. The Denny Wayne was a true Key West original! It was locally built by a guy named Ron, who was evidently quite a creative constructor. The boat was twenty-six feet long by nine feet wide. It had a forward compartment, AKA... "Florida Room". The walls folded out and provided a view of the area around the craft. On the floor was a hatch that when uncovered, provided an opening to squeeze through directly into the sea. It was also a great place to drop a fishing line with hopes of catching dinner.

A variety of fish and lobster dwelled beneath the Denny Wayne. Aft of the "Florida Room" was a door opening into the main living quarters. On the door was a plaque that read, "Screw Room". Many a chuckle was elicited from that marine bawdiness. In the cabin was a bunk elevated four feet off of the floor, a table and cooking stove of the Coleman variety. At the end of the bunk was a tub for bathing in water heated on the stove. Another remarkable feature was located under the floorboard of the room. When the board was removed, it revealed a three-foot by two-foot clear plexiglass panel, a window to the deep! Truly a glass bottom boat, it was. When I placed a spotlight on it at night; fish, squid and the resident small octopus that lived on the barnacled, crusty hull of the boat would appear and feed in the proper pecking order. It was hypnotic to see the frenzied swirl of eat or be eaten taking place inches from our faces.

The anchorage location was damn near as unique as the Denny Wayne, which by the way, I named after my little brother. The boat was located between Sigsbee and Fleming Keys. Five hundred yards east of the houseboat and a few acres in size was, Rat Key. Rat Key was created when the U.S. Navy dredged a channel back in the day. My houseboat was anchored at the end of that channel. Depending on which way the wind was blowing, the depth under the Denny Wayne was either

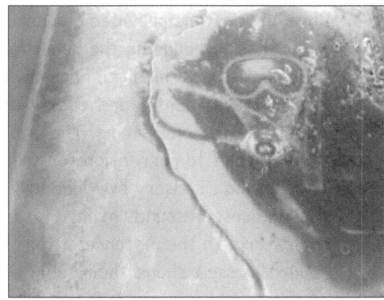

Captain Mike Fulmer looking up through glass bottom of Denny Wayne

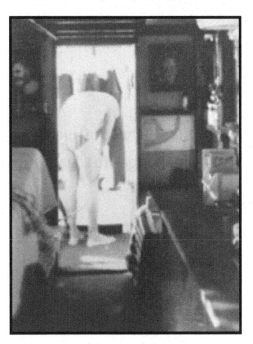

Rinsing dive gear.

four feet, or twenty feet. This change of depth was remarkable. The sheer face of the carved coral trench was a habitat for lobster, crab and fish of every sort. The first lobster season on the site was very productive. Five of us caught our limit on the first day. We gorged on the tasty creatures along with crab and all the condiments and supplemental dishes. My 'ol sea dog, Hobbit, also had his fill of the catch. I imagine his Purina barely fit the bill after the cur sampled tasty treats from the ocean. He was a good 'ol dog, one of my best furry friends.

113

While the daytime provided a panoramic view of the ocean and many islands surrounding the houseboat, the night cranked the exhilaration up to quasi-magical. From my raft, the stars blazed and the boat swayed gently, or fiercely, on the end of the anchor chain like a June-bug on a string. The entire rooftop was an open deck and lent itself to perfection for grilling, swilling and kicking back experiencing a sensory overload of the sights and unseen sounds of my aquatic backyard. In the distance, other "live-a-board" vessels shone their cabin lights of candle and electric. Different genres of music could be heard faintly emanating from my fellow sea dwellers. Conversations of every nature would occasionally be heard. Most of it was laughter, some was cursing and screams of passion too. Then the wind changed direction, all the vocal distraction would wisp away until the next bout of southerly wind brought forth the sounds of humanity to my salty ears.

Resting between Atocha and Margarita sites.

Each time I left for an expedition to the **Atocha/Margarita** sites, I had to bid the boat farewell for a week or two. I did what I could to secure it to lessen the chance of pirates coming aboard and doing their thievery. I left a radio blaring rock and roll and a cabin light on. The boat's batteries were constantly being recharged by a solar panel which afforded plenty of power for my improvised security of lights and sound. I padlocked the doors and on occasion, I left a stuffed dummy of sorts complete with a hat in the bunk. With these precautions and my fellow "live-a-board" neighbors keeping an eye out, the system worked well. Each time I arrived back in Key West from sea, I was relieved when I went through the opening at Garrison Bight and saw the boat a mile away, floating intact and proud. Marauders and storms alike left him untouched each time. My raft waited

patiently beckoning me to clamor aboard, have a cold one and contemplate the next adventure to come. We will revisit the Denny Wayne later, Sam. It looks like we are going back to Hannibal!

Hambone

Lobster harvest.
Photo: Michael Fulmer

Dear Sam,

Life is slowing down for me now. The swimming season is coming to a halt. My part time work as a "swimming pool man" is almost over. As it stands now, I have only four pools still in operation. I service them on Wednesdays. That gives me six days off in between to catch up on domestic duties and projects such as returning to Hannibal to scratch around your yard, and the sunken riverboat here at the Cape. The boat is currently twenty feet underwater. Last month the river dropped within a few feet of exposing it. I fully expect to be able to examine it in the coming month. If I can at least extract one of the batteries from it revealed last year, and...find a manufacturing date, it would be a satisfying season. Excuse me for rambling. My point is this; I get to retire until April and pursue interests other than the mighty dollar.

Sam, I fully intended to write and send this message after my next trip to Hannibal, but something amazing has happened. Message number nine has been found downstream at Point Pleasant, Missouri, and very remarkable ties exists between you and the town! Since I began this message, I've been to Hannibal and I did indeed make a huge find on your old homestead. I will cover the trip and the find in the next letter. I feel that I should report on the finding of message nine first.

I hurled message number nine in the Mississippi last spring when the river was running deep and swift. Before it was found

last week, it traveled at least a hundred miles and then a few. When you consider the twists and turns of the "Big Muddy", I think my estimate of how far it sailed is conservative. While I would prefer for a discovered message to be found at a much greater distance from Cape Girardeau, mileage wise, the second found message made it a lot farther than the one young Dawson stumbled across in Hannibal.

When I heard news of the discovery of number nine, I was at Capaha Park playing a round of disc golf on a fine summer's day. Deb informed me via phone of the discovery. The discoverer, upon seeing the contact information, called my home phone. In a distracted state, I finished my game. I drove home in an excited state, anticipating calling the finder of the message. When I called the number, a man answered the phone. I explained who I was and thanked him for notifying me that he'd found the message. He informed me that he didn't actually discover the bottle. An elderly couple had found it lodged in the woods at Point Pleasant. As the swollen river receded, the bottle was stranded in a thicket up the river bank. After reading the introductory letter part of the message and perusing the letter itself, the couple decided they didn't want to contact me. Hopefully, future reviews of our spectral correspondence will be a bit more encouraging! They turned the bottle and contents over to the gentleman who called me. He was interested enough to fill me in about the discovery. After a brief conversation, I thanked the man again and asked permission to call him back in a few days for a more formal interview. This also gave me time to begin researching Point Pleasant, Missouri for any parallels between you and the village. I wasn't disappointed with the results of the inquiry. The first connection revealed between you and the landing place of message number nine was pretty cool. The second one was major. It blew me out of the water.

Sam, in **"Notebook, 1898"**, you spoke of love this way..."When you fish for love, bait with your heart, not your brain." At the port of Point Pleasant, you did just that. I have to wonder if your act of love at Point Pleasant was on you mind when you cited amorousness in the notebook.

Before being smitten by Olivia, you had strong feelings for others. One in particular is the reason for my rant about Point Pleasant. Nancy Miriam Robbins, or Myra...as she was referred to, could well have been the one you would have married if not for circumstances of obstacles that voided any chance of matrimony. Myra was the focus of your heart when you piloted the mighty Mississippi. The efforts you made to pursue her ended up in a sort of unrequited love. Futile and fruitless was your amorous campaign.

Chores summon me, Sam. In the next message I will continue the story of the discovery of message number nine. You will be pleased to hear it. So will Miss Myra...

Hambone

118

Dear Sam,

It occurred to me this morning that I've been writing to you for over a year. From the inauguration of this project, I have figured it will take at least fifty messages to complete the effort. I reckon I have another year to go before I'm finished. There's still a lot more I need to share with you, and who knows what will be added, when suddenly revealed. Speaking of surprise revelations, let's get back to message nine and it's romance of love denied.

Nancy Miriam Robbins, (Myra), was truly the belle of the ball. Her beauty was widely renown, as were her charms. Myra was the only daughter of Susan and James Robbins. At 24 Olive Street, in St. Louis...James, along with William Bowen, owned an eating establishment. I've not been able to find the address on contemporary maps. Olive Street begins on the 200th block today, and extends to the West. Cities change...and time changes, everything changes except creation. Your first meeting with the most delightful Myra could well have been at her father's chophouse. The eatery was near the river you launched from and docked at hundreds of times during your all too brief piloting years. I'm sure that James and William, (a former resident of our beloved Hannibal), served up fine fare.

When Eads Bridge, the first bridge to span the Mississippi at St. Louis, was dedicated on July 4, 1874...Miss Myra was the, "Belle of the ball", as recollected by Mrs. June Ransburg in the

October 21st or 22nd edition of the New Madrid, Missouri's, **Daily Record.** Mrs. Ransburg was Myra's great, great niece. An estimated 200,000 turned out for the grand affair. All day long brass bands trumpeted the joyous occasion. Miss Myra Robbins evidently had the beauty and characteristics as a debutante diplomat for the steel and marble span joining the east and west riverbanks, like I'm telling you something you don't already know, Sam!

Your attraction to Myra was professed in words and action. Upon returning to St. Louis after a voyage, gifts for her from New Orleans were not unheard of. Another gesture you made was remarkable, chivalrous and risky, and...has everything to do with the discovery of message number nine!

You came ashore at Point Pleasant, Missouri, just as message number nine did. After tying up, you sent Myra a lovely decorated cake that was made by the ships cook. You 'ol dog you...a hopeless romantic. A captain stays with his ship and evidently a river pilot stays with his boat. Thanks to my experience with the sunken riverboat here at the Cape, I learned quickly from an archaeologist not to refer to sunken riverboats as sunken ships.

As the porter disappeared over the hill on his way to see Myra and to deliver the sweet treat, I have to wonder if your heart yearned to be the deliverer. Miss Myra was staying at the Robbins Farm at Point Pleasant for a short visit. That was some real chivalry, Sam, docking there to convey your admiration for Miss Robbins. You brought thousands of tons of steel, wood and belching steam to a pause for your love. To deliver a cake. Nice style my friend.

When Myra returned to St. Louis, you decided to make it official and ask her father permission to court her. I was sorry to hear that James Robbins refused permission saying that, "He did not approve of river men!" Ouch. As late as 1867 you had dreams of Myra. In a letter to William Bowen, dated, June 7, 1867, you wrote, "How is Miriam?. Tell her I dream of her still. And I dream of Mrs. Robbins too, but not so much. Good bye, my oldest friend."

I love it that message number nine washed up in Point Pleasant. I never would have known of the love between you and Nancy Miriam Robbins, the princess of Eads Bridge. I requested from and received the October 21st or 22nd, 1960 story of your calling on Myra at Point Pleasant. The headline read, "Mark Twain pays court to Miss Myra Robbins at Point Pleasant." That's an understatement. As I quoted you...you were..."fishing for love", with cake as the bait!

Deb tossing message # 9.

As I was checking my log today, I discovered I hadn't thrown bottle number nine. My Deb did the honor for me. The love of my life floated the message to Point Pleasant. How fitting. We are pleased. I hope you and Myra are, as well as Pleasant Hannibal Clemens' your older brother who died at three months...Goodnight, Sam...

Hambone

Message Twenty-seven...
"Huck's Yard"
October 14, 2014
Cape Girardeau, Mo.

Dear Sam,

As I pulled into Hannibal last month I was fired up. A narrow window of opportunity had opened up to return to the surrounding property of your boyhood home. The weather was perfect for digging and the earth relatively soft. Obligations, both personal and business, were either caught up with or quartered on the back burners. My plan was to stay in Hannibal two nights and search for two and a half days. With fall coming soon and the cold, wet windy days it can bring, I knew this was my last expedition of 2014. I wanted to make the most of the effort that these old bones could produce. My plan was to widen the search and recheck areas already scanned for artifacts associated with your tenure at 206-208 Hill Street. So far, the collection from your yard contains fifty or so items. A few are spectacular. Some are interesting, but the rest of the assortment of crusty finds are of no interest but hard to let go of just yet. It must be the pack-rat in me that causes me to hoard worthless scrap items for a while.

By the time I checked into my lodgings, unpacked gear and ate a late lunch, it was around 2 p.m. which left me enough daylight to search four more hours. As I sat on the stoop in front of the hotel, I made a plan. Behind your old house, as you know, is the historical Blankenship property complete with a newly constructed structure that represents the old dwelling of Huck Finn...Tom Blankenship. I decided to start there. In the past I'd only searched your property, keeping in mind to take a look-see at the

122

Finn property, too. This was the chance to do it. I had imagined you leaving through your bedroom window many times at night as a result of Tom beckoning you with a catcall or whistle for a night of adventures as Hannibal slept. I'm sure you boys beat a path between the two properties. Being curious, I also wondered what the two of you might have dropped in the night that could still be under the soil waiting for the proper sweep of my humming detector.

I picked up my five gallon bucket containing accessories for the hunt, the backpack and metal detector. Then, I walked down Hill Street past your home and cut through the east garden, passing through the gate of the stone wall built by the WPA in 1937. To this day the wall is in splendid shape, complete with buttresses that will guarantee the stability of the massive structure for decades to come unless an earthquake strikes. I think the structure will survive a fairly strong tremor. With the builders of the depression era being so grateful to have a job, they built it to match their heart and spirit which gushed with steadfastness and strength.

Keeping myself focused on the plan, I entered the backyard of the Huck Finn property. It was tempting to stop along the way and search a few undetected spots at your home. I didn't. I completed a visual survey of the Huck Finn Home trying to figure out where to start. One problem I'd encountered in the past was fill-dirt which has been laid down in several areas adding modern layers of earth over the virgin soil of your era. The practice added more distance between the artifacts I seek and the coil of the metal detector. It also slows down the process due to the time consumed discovering and digging of items I have no interest in, such as soda caps, foil, coins, fasteners and other modern scrap. I have to reach the depth you and your family trod on, and then a bit deeper. If I had to make an educated guess, the soil that **naturally** built up at your homestead since your departure from Hannibal has raised the level of dirt in the yard by eight to twelve inches, depending on its specific topography.

While scoping-out Huck's yard, I saw an ill-defined depression in the yard that should be devoid of any modern fill. I decided to start there. I unpacked my backpack in the shade of the small tree next to the chosen spot. On a towel I placed a trowel, notebook, tape measure and GPS unit. Within a minute after exclaiming, "Today's the day!", I was waving the detector over the ground and advancing slowly away from the tree. Five minutes into the search, my detector came to life indicating with a loud beep that I'd pinpointed something metallic. I pushed a wooden marker into the spot, leaned my detector against the tree, turned on my handheld pin-pointer and dug a divot with my trowel around the marker. Hoping for an easy dig and an item of historical importance, I flipped the plug over and peered into the hole. I saw nothing...which is typical. I was going to have to work more for it, so I pointed my pin-pointer into the hole. Nothing registered on it. I gently probed the hole with a thin phillips screwdriver and felt it touch nothing. Next, I removed more dirt from the hole.

This time the pin-pointer beeped when I held it against the bottom of the excavation indicating the find was only a few more inches deep. Using a small brush, I removed the fill-dirt left in the hole. I looked in the hole and there in the bottom of the hole was a really cool little buckle with a green patina looking oh so sweet! It looked old. It was old. I was in virgin dirt! After a cursory look at the artifact, I placed it on the spread out towel and took a GPS measurement of the coordinates of the hole. After triangulating the dig with a tape measure from fixed points on the perimeter, I filled the hole back in after rechecking it. I replaced the grass plug and tidied

up around the hole. For good measure I threw a few leaves on it as well. It was darn near impossible to tell I dug there. That's the way to do it. Leave no traces.

   Digging on the other hits resulted in the finding of a square fastener, a plumb-bob looking thingy, some bits of iron and what

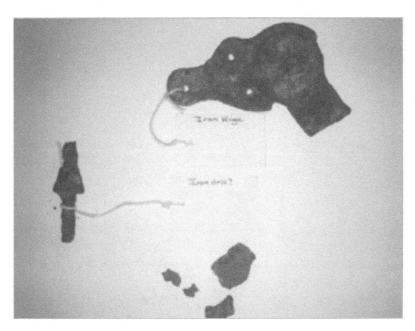

appeared to be a small jointed armature off of a trunk lid or something. Although I'd dug only four or five holes, time was running out for the day's work. The sun was setting, my bones were aching and my belly grumbling. I decided to call it quits for the day. I packed up my gear and finds and ambled up Hill Street with my detector over my shoulder. After stopping on the stoop of the hotel for a smoke, I went to my room to drop off my load. I washed, unloaded my bike from my van and went to old Hannibal town in search of a thick, dark beer and supper. That was a success.

As I sat at an outside table quaffing and eating, I thought about the buckle I'd found. Beneath the crud I'd seen some scrollwork and numbers pressed into it. After eating, I sat at my table and had another beer. As I rubbernecked at passing cars and tourists, I made a plan to go back to my hotel, soak in the spa, swim and clean the buckle for an identification attempt. All these plans went well, even the identification of the buckle! I will get into that in my next message. I ended up very pleased with the buckle. Little did I know of the treasure to come! Goodnight, Sam.

Hambone.

Dear Sam,

After a soaking in warm water and a gentle brushing, the scrollwork and numbers on the buckle were revealed with the aid of my magnifying glass and some decent lighting. The numbers were a patent date, September 2, 1856. I searched the patent date at the U.S. Patent website and immediately learned all about the device. It is a suspender buckle. It was patented by Edward Parker of Plymouth, Connecticut, patent number US15666A. Part of Mr. Parker's description of the buckle is as follows, "My invention consisting of striking or swaging the bow and loop in one piece from a metal plate and securing the tongue there in by bending the center cross piece which divides the bow and loop around the shank of the tongue, as will be presently described. The mode of construction is extremely simple and a durable and economical buckle is obtained thereby."

One of the prongs of the buckle is missing. There is a dent in the frame of the buckle where the prong would normally rest. I wonder if the buckle was lost through some sort of sudden act or trauma or did the wearer lose it due to continued use after the prong went missing? We will never know how it was lost, or who lost it. We can only speculate.

Woodson Blankenship was born in South Carolina in 1799. Woodson was the father of Tom Blankenship, aka, Huck Finn. Tom's father appears in the 1850 Hannibal census. I haven't found any documentation to place him in Hannibal beyond the 1850 record. Also, I haven't found out what year he died. Is it plausible the buckle was dropped by Woodson, perhaps in one of his well documented alcohol-fueled benders? Probably not. Even if Woodson had occupied the property after the patent date on the buckle, many others lived and worked on the property after the Blankenship's left. I do know that. The spot where I found it is a stone's throw from the sawmill behind your home. Maybe one of the workmen lost it. Blankenship worked at the sawmill, too. It's said, if he had money jingling in his pocket, it immediately went for drink. It's a great artifact. No matter who lost it. Hell, if we're going to speculate, we can wonder just as well if Tom Blankenship lost it himself. Sure would be cool to have a suspender buckle of Huck Finn's. Now, that's treasure!

After a full country breakfast I trudged down Hill Street early the next morning, gear in hand. The memory of the buckle was still fresh yet fading as I entered the courtyard on the east side of your home. While the exploring and recoveries at Huck's yesterday were exciting enough, I was glad to be on your turf and had high hopes for a major discovery. The day was going to be spent on the grounds of your boyhood home. Although yesterday's search of the Finn property was productive, I feel I should be on your property since the core mission is to recover a trace of you. The trip to Hannibal from the Cape takes around four hours and the lodging and essentials are out of my pocket. I try to milk my expenses, time and effort as much as possible while I'm in Hannibal. Other than the Blankenship dig the day before, I have stuck to your boyhood home.

After six hours of searching, pin-pointing, digging and a little cussing...my take for the day was; a modern quarter and penny, one square nail, one piece of wire, a modern nail, a large tack and a half dozen pieces of modern refuse, I spent a lot of time yanking it all from the earth. Aside from the hand-forged square nail, I had nothing to show for a precious day's work. There was still four hours of daylight left but very little light left in me. Hunger, heat, old age and frustration had taken their toll. I was dehydrated too. Although I had used every trick in the book to find treasure from controlled overlapping sweeps of the detector coil to wild-catting and walking aimlessly, a good find eluded me. I sat and leaned against the inside of the whitewashed fence, slugged some water and rested. As "Twainiac touristas" walked by, they paid no notice of me...nor I to them. I daydreamed about you and Tom, thought about Mel and napped for a few minutes.

With a slight startle...I came out of my stupor. I slowly got up to the sound of my bones and tendons popping like corn. I was stove-in even worse. Before long I was heading back to my room, head hanging and filled with disappointed. Even though sunset wasn't for a few more hours, I knew I was spent. "Today wasn't the day," I muttered. Sometimes you have to regroup, rest and eat. This was one of those instances. I ate,

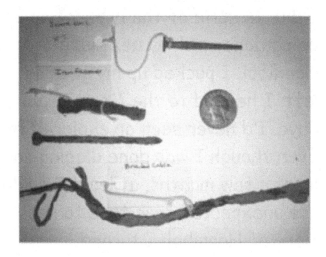

swam and soaked. Tomorrow will be another day...   Hambone

Dear Sam,

After a solid seven hours of dreamless replenishing slumber, I returned to the grounds on Hill Street hoping my last day in Hannibal would be a productive one. I was planning to leave in twenty-four hours. My brother Henry was expecting me at his home for a bar-b-cue. I wanted to get to his house early. Leaving Hannibal early would make it possible to see my family in Park Hills, Missouri on the way back to Cape Girardeau.

If you want to know what I found that day after five hours of searching, refer to message twenty eight. I found nothing of interest! Once again, modern junk was the take. Sam...sometimes we have to know when to back-off, and...back-off I did. In spite of the implication of being done until my next visit to Hannibal, I packed up my gear and left. I headed to the Mark Twain Cave. I'd never seen or explored it. Even though I was done digging for at least a few months, at least I could use unexpected free time to see more of Hannibal. I turned, "tourista".

The tour of the cave and the performance of my good friend's impersonation of you were fantabulous! I felt steeped and surrounded by history in the cool, well-lit grottos underground. I understand why your signature on the cave walls has yet to be found. I was told there are at least a quarter million autographs scratched in the walls of that marvelous underworld. The hope was dashed quickly that I would waltz in and find your name. To do that would be a "holy grail find"! The signatures are on every height and level and in all reachable nooks and crannies. It was cool to walk the same paths you did in your youth. With enough imagination, Injun Joe's spectral form could be easily conjured-up, lurking at the limits of the illumination.

With the cave scratched-off my bucket list, I headed back to Hannibal with another stop in mind of which to tour. As I pulled into the old Hannibal cemetery, I immediately began searching, hoping to find your family plot. I was going in cold without direction but I wanted to pay respect to your family. Slowly I circled the boneyard twice on it's narrow gravel road. The Clemens' name on the weathered tombstones plainly evaded me. I did get out of the Atlantis van in order to take a closer look at a Hawkins' family plot. Finding Laura Hawkins, AKA...Becky Thatcher's place of rest, would have been exciting, too. I didn't find her. I know her married name. Had the stop not been spur of the moment, a little research would have taken me straight to the graves. I'm fairly sure it was the right graveyard, though I failed in my quest. The time of solitude at the final resting place of Hannibal's earliest citizenry invigorated me. Only the dead and I existed for awhile. These boney artifacts whispered a message indiscernible in any hole at the boyhood home. It was a message of not giving up, for win or lose, your final destination is here.

After leaving the cemetery I made a short stop at the high cliff south of Hannibal. What a great view from the lofty perch also known as, "lover's leap". The view of Hannibal and the river is a sight to behold. As I took-in the view, I wondered about the name of the place and if any townspeople had ever jumped to certain death. I pondered about the grave-sites I'd visited and if any of those passed souls used this height as a portal to their plot. I need to look that up.

When I arrived back at my hotel I decided to take another bike ride. The last ride I took had been enjoyable and gave me an opportunity to poke my nose into interesting alleys, side streets and other places made less intimate by being in my van. I rode north along a street beside the river for a few miles. I came across the railroad bridge, admired it and then headed back to town. By then I was tired and hungry. I rode along the riverfront and came across the Mark Twain Riverboat. Their bulletin board advertised a dinner cruise in a few hours. I was immediately sold on the idea.

Two hours later I was aboard the boat and seated at my table. The food was excellent and the beer dark and cold. I went to the top deck and stood just below the wheelhouse to take-in the view. As I puffed a smoke and reflected on the fact that all I had found was a great buckle, a hinge and a bunch of junk this trip, I knew I had to try again in the morning. If I started early enough, I could still make it to Henry's for a visit and search for three hours. I'm glad I did...   Hambone

Dear Sam,

Happy 179th birthday! I hope it's a good one. The past year has passed quickly. It feels like your last birthday was only a few months ago. Relating the story of Comet Ison on your birthday last year still feels very fresh.

In your autobiography you wrote about impossibility and said... "Apparently, there is nothing that cannot happen." I didn't have the quote in mind as I stumbled down Hill Street packing my gear in a sleep induced early morning fog. As anticipated, I had around three hours to search and dig before heading south to Henry's for the family bar-b-cue. I rarely see my beloved blood family. There was no way I was going to miss seeing them no matter how empty handed I was at the expiration of my extended time. The chance of finding a major artifact verged on impossibility. I'd pretty much chalked the trip as a bust. After a year of researching and planning, it appeared my one and only search of 2014 was hexed. Ominous storm clouds lurked over Hannibal. An occasional heavy mist and isolated showers were impacting the region. I don't mind being cold and wet but, once a deluge of rain starts...all digging ceases. The wet earth causes my detector and pin-pointer to change in their accuracy. Digging becomes a sloppy mess making it difficult to conceal any holes dug in vain.

I entered the east courtyard and laid my gear out at the picnic table next to the WPA wall. Luckily, the batteries in my electronics were still at nearly a full charge. Not having to put in fresh ones gained me another fifteen minutes of searching and excavating. I hadn't picked out a specific spot to detect, yet I did have a specific area in mind. The plan was to start at the edge of the boyhood home and work east. Even though I'd worked the area before, one never knows what could have been missed. At least this plan snugged me up to the very foundation of the house. Removal of some shrubbery since my last 2013 effort made access easier for the task at hand.

Within five minutes of scanning the dirt, my detector lit up with a loud shrill. My location was only a few feet from the home's southeast corner. After a few minutes of pin-pointing the metallic target, I shoved a marker into the dirt. I had only a couple of hours left. At this time, pin-pointing the target was crucial in order to avoid time lost because of fruitless digging. Targets can be elusive even when care is taken to pin-point carefully. Fifteen minutes later I was still digging and probing with my pin-pointer. Forty-five minutes passed. The hole was now six inches wide and eight inches deep. The object I sought was causing me stress and many choice words. I considered abandoning the spot and moving along to another. I could mark the spot and retry it next year in favor of another, more shallow hit. I thought about Mel and Treasure Salvors Inc. never giving up. I stayed with the hole and dug more. At the depth of around nine inches, the pin-pointer indicated the elusive metal in the wall of the hole. I dug parallel to the ground in the direction of your home. The hole was now forming an L-shape as I dug, pin-pointed and dug some more. With only an hour left I went full bore with the dig. I was determined to extract the artifact whether it be a nail or an amazing discovery.

Another thirty minutes passed. I was up to my elbow in the L-shaped hole. The pin-pointer registered strongly, beeping and vibrating. I took my glove off and probed blindly with my bare hand. I felt an object that was not rock or bits of wood. It was metal. I pulled on it. It would not budge. Sightlessly I dug around it in an effort to dislodge it. Steadfast it stayed. I backed-off, had a smoke and figured out what to do. I walked a block to my vehicle and retrieved my pliers. Very carefully I gripped the edge of the metal and began to wiggle it out of it's resting place. After a couple minutes of careful manipulation, the artifact came free. I do hope that no one was within earshot to hear my expletives when I saw what the object really was. It was unidentifiable iron scrap useless to the endeavor and a total waste of the time invested when time was of critical importance. To add insult to injury, thunder cracked in the distance and a heavy rain came down. I scurried to protect my gear and equipment and retreated to the picnic table cussing along the way. I rarely get so worked up. I do have a temper but long ago I shoved it under to be buried. Things looked up a bit when the rain suddenly stopped. At least I could rescan the hole and cover it back up as attractively as possible. There wasn't enough time to repair the damage I'd done to the lawn, and...detect any further. I rescanned the hole to hell. The detector remained quiet. A quick scan with the hand probe produced no results. The scrap I'd found was the only metal to retrieve. I probed with my bare hand in the recesses of the dig. A lump was at my fingertips. I pulled my flashlight out of the backpack and examined as far back as I could see into the void. I saw something ceramic. When I wiggled the pottery shard from the wall of the hole, pieces of coal and bits of old glass tumbled out also. Although I immediately suspected I had stumbled across a refuse pile, that fantasy was confirmed by the rest of the objects wrenched free of the dirt. Five pieces of ceramic that fit together as a jigsaw revealed it to be the lip of an old bowl! Thin white glazed pieces of

Discovery of refuse area / Photo: Karen Pfister

ceramic that probably were once a tea or coffee cup were revealed! Five small chunks of coal were part of the collection! Six bits of brick came next. Three pieces of glass were retrieved without cutting my fingers. A chunk of coal slag presented itself. Three chunks of brown glazed ceramic rounded-off the honey hole. They looked like bowl fragments. In the final minutes of my precious few hours, success was made! A nice "tourista family" I talked to earlier shot a few images of me digging with glee. Cussing had been replaced by whistling. A sudden rumble from

Photo: Karen Pfister

overhead preceded a heavy downpour. In the rain and wind I did my best to refill the hole. The dirt I'd piled on a towel began to run like molasses into the finely manicured grass. As I hastily took care of the business at hand, I knew there were more buried objects.

Time was up, weather was up and I was up. What a score!

I look forward to returning to Hannibal in 2015 to dig at the same spot. If I hadn't found the piece of worthless metal, I wouldn't have found the remarkable and diverse collection. Whether it's a refuse pile of discarded everyday items, or the privy...either one is a trove of items and information. This spot is either a minor or major window to the past. We shall see. I did find an 1854 map of the property showing a small structure resembling a privy. Items of every sort have been found in outhouses. Some thrown in after useful service, some dropped, and some hidden. I will grid the location off next year and go purely archaeological. I am not blowing it! One goal of the project is to demonstrate that treasure hunters and archaeologists can work together for mutual benefit. Oh, by the way...the bar-b-cue at Henry's was excellent! My family enjoyed seeing the collection. Goodnight, Sam...

Hambone

First artifacts from the refuse area.

Dear Sam,

I'm back. A wave of sickness bullied through the house. Deb and I are healthy again. Although the affliction was merely a cut and dried common cold, the symptoms were bad enough to keep me inside taking lazy to such an extreme that even you would have admired and strove to imitate. I did do a bit of reading and exercised my fork and spoon skills to the hilt. How does it go? "Feed a fever and starve a cold?" Or, is it vice versa? I couldn't get it straight. As a precaution...I fed the cold and fed the fever. It certainly didn't hurt. I'm much better now and finally coming around.

I'm not sure which direction to take on this letter. The possibilities are numerous. We can go back to the Cape Girardeau Wreck, Key West, Hannibal, or a few spots in between. It's a hard decision to make. Either direction, there's a lot more to cover. I try my best to keep it all straight and comprehensive. The content of these pages is simple. My biggest challenge is to present these messages in the proper progression while keeping all the dots connected. Hopefully I'm not trying too little or too hard.

After a nine month wait, the river has receded enough to expose the wreck here. In a few hours I'll be on-site investigating it. As luck would have it, the weather outside is drizzling with a threatening ice storm and a temperature of twenty-five degrees. Layered clothing, a sock hat, gloves and my rubber boots will ward-off most of the cold precipitation and mud.

Although this expedition is intended to be just a look-see, I will take a backpack with assorted tools and electronics just in case. I'd rather have some gear and not need it rather than vice-versa. At best, half of the **Amy Elizabeth** will be revealed. The ten foot level is still three feet short of revealing her totally. I am a bit pumped to find out how much the erosion of the boat in the past months has brought to light. I expect something cool and historic. Every visit to her produces something new. Any digging on her will be very difficult today. I expect the riverbank to be frozen solid. We shall see.

Sam...it's now later in the afternoon. A few hours ago I took a break from writing and headed down to the river to see what the months of erosion have revealed on the wreck. The drizzle of rain, mixed with a few sleet pellets, was tolerable in my chosen

clothing. Instead of parking downtown to obtain access to the river, plus a half mile walk...I chose to park at Honker's Boat Dock, walk across the railroad trestle and hike a few hundred yards. My good friend, Calvin Brennan, joined me. The treacherous nature of the final trek down the bank to the wreck-site makes it a good idea to have assistance. I've lost my footing several times and tumbled onto the rocks. Today was especially slippery with the rain and ice

covering the bank.

As I made my way down to the wreck I saw the large cleat on the wreck exposed along with some other structural components. As I stood over her bones, I was dismayed to see silt covered it over to the level of when she was first discovered over two years ago. I cussed a bit and took photographs. Fortunately, the stern of the forlorn craft was still exposed. As you know, the stern is the current area of interest. That's where the batteries are stored. I have permission from the Missouri Department of Natural Resources to dig one out, examine it, photograph it and then put it back as I found it. Although I packed my backpack with basic equipment, I didn't attempt any excavation. The silt was frozen and conditions were not agreeable.

As we made our way back up the slippery bank, we kept our eyes peeled for any artifacts washed out of the riverbank.

Halfway up the slope I spotted a rounded piece of clear glass sticking out of the wet dirt. As I attempted to yank it from it's resting place, I fully expected it to be a broken shard. Intact glass items are a bit rare. Much to my surprise, the item came out intact and undamaged. It was a small ink bottle. It had no chips or cracks.

At this time I have assigned it's era of manufacture to around 1940, maybe older. It has no seams that would indicate that it's machine made. If it is a hand-blown bottle, it could be turn of the century. I will let you know the final approximate date.

I considered cleaning the ink bottle of the mud that fills and coats it. For the time being, I'm leaving it untouched. It tells a better story in it's original condition. I'll leave cleaning it up to you, should you come for it. Ha...

Hambone

Dear Sam,

    Although the temperature outside is a mere forty-five degrees, it is an improvement over the twenty degree chill we've experienced over the past week or so. The slight increase in temperature caused me to think of spring and summer. That led my thinking to Key West where summer is eternal. Pondering Key West led to thoughts about the Atocha. All things considered, let's go back to Key West and revisit treasure...

    Although I've relayed some of my experiences as a diver salvaging Mel's, *Nuestra Senora de Atocha,* I haven't shared with you the massive preparations we made that eventually lead up to a fella strapping on scuba-tanks and diving for real Spanish sunken treasure. There's a lot more required of a treasure diver than metal detecting and hand-fanning the deep for artifacts, gold, silver and emeralds.

    Our team performed every laborious task needed to maintain and support the salvage vessels and anything else associated with our salty expeditions. Boats require copious sums of blood, sweat and labor. It's not natural to mix steel, wood, wiring, machinery and fuel with water, especially saltwater and it's supercharged corrosive properties. The sea takes it's toll on boats. Of all the tasks we performed, boat maintenance consumed our time more than any other duties. It wasn't unheard of to be in dry-dock for months, and the hellish situation that place can become. Not to mention that all the while, other boats were reporting their latest gilded finds suffering our conditions even more. Welding, painting, scraping, sanding, hammering and many other torturous duties were our fate. Usually, a boatyard trip occurred in the zenith of summer in the lower keys where the heat and humidity caused your body to become a magnet for air-born rust and ground paint.

Banishment to the boat-yard for repairs and maintenance always hung over our shoulders. That, is why we did all we could to stay out of the clutches of that particular predicament. We maintained our boats and equipment at the docks in the highest of mechanical and preserved condition. The regimen of care started immediately after we tied up. Upon arrival from the treasure site, no matter how exhausted, burned and cut-up we were from the trip...our floating treasure factory was immediately hosed several times to rinse off the salt that was eating away at all organics and metal. Trash was hauled to the dumpster and lists were made of repairs to tend to and supplies to procure if we wanted to get back on the booty trail within a few days. The Captain would appear on the dock above us and tell us whether we had a

The Swordfish in the clutches of the boatyard.

day off the next day, or...to inform us what time to show up the next day. Then, we'd lug all the treasure and artifacts to his vehicle. Next, he would take the bounty to the Mel Fisher Museum and turn it over to the conservators. Exceptional finds might find themselves on Mel's desk immediately for his delight, still smelling of the sea.

If we left the wharf within three days of time in port, it was a quick turn-around. In the days leading up to sailing, the salvage boat was a frenzy of activity. The boat was examined stem to stern to identify any maintenance needed. There was always plenty to do; from cleaning the fuel cartridges, to stripping and painting weathered wood and steel. Oil changes were done on most of the motors we counted on from generators to scuba and deck air-compressors. All the while, fingers were crossed that we wouldn't find any major malfunctions which would require a sentence to the dreaded boat-yard. Although most of us were in a semi-fog induced state by the previous evening of revelry in Key West, we performed our tasks equally and without error. Our meager paychecks wouldn't last long in port. A quick turn-around benefitted our bank accounts. While at sea, all quantities of food and equipment were provided by Mel's Treasure Salvors, Inc. We enjoyed excellent devices to perform our work with and sustenance to fuel our bodies with the protein and calories we needed to crew and dive on the ocean.

On the morning of departure, several crewman would head to the grocery with a very long list of food and staples needed to supply a crew of five for the duration of a week to ten days. We'd often end up with a train of seven carts filled to the brim. After the clerk tallied the bill, we filled out a check signed by

Mel. Eight hundred dollars was a typical amount. This was in 1985-89. One could easily double the total in today's money. We hauled all the goods to the dock where the whole crew would form a line like a bucket brigade, allowing for an efficient delivery. Perishable foodstuffs were consolidated in a walk-in ice bunker in order of when they would be consumed during the expedition. Lockers were stuffed with the boxed and canned items and securely fastened. Equipment was lashed to the deck in case of rough seas or wakes from passing ships.

After the captain or mate warmed the twin diesels for awhile, we heaved off the lines and set ourselves free of the island. The first part of the excursion was a mere one hundred yards to the fuel dock where we took-on hundreds of gallons of diesel and pumped ice into our food locker through an extendable eight inch wide hose. The excitement was contagious as we left the fuel dock. Days of preparation had panned out. Every task, whether mundane or interesting, was done. Fully loaded for bear, the crew and ship were pointed south by southwest for a twenty-six mile, four hour cruise to the Marquesas Islands where off her shores lay the golden bones we desperately sought, the remains of that broken...yet proud galleon, **Atocha.**

Once we cleared Key West Harbor, I rarely looked back as it disappeared over the horizon. All of our love's, lusts and vices were now abandoned as we crawled along in our sluggish workboat. The boats were not the speediest, however...they efficiently filled the role of being our platform. When anchored over a suspected treasure spot, they dug ample holes with their mailboxes, (excavators), as well as any other on the planet. As we crept along, there were still jobs to do besides ride and enjoy the scenery and

145

dream of treasure. Scuba tanks had to be filled from the cranky diesel compressor. Gear, both personal and work related, was placed in its allotted precious space. Bunks were claimed and made

Ham's hands on cover of Life Magazine, March, 1987

up with bedding freshly unpacked from then Margaret Truman Laundry in Key West. With personal and work gear deployed, along with other jobs accomplished, it wasn't unusual to take in the rest of the voyage from the bow or crowded into the wheelhouse, a' smokin and a' jokin'.

More later, Sam. I need to keep my gills wet. Heading for a swim. I'll continue this story in message thirty-three. Goodnight....

Hambone

Message Thirty-three...
"Crewing the Virgalona"
January 25, 2015
Cape Girardeau, Mo.

Dear Sam,

Key West slips over the horizon when the distance to the Atocha is half traveled. The ever present chain of islands off to starboard are evident all the way to the Marquesas. The Spaniards camped on the island while salvaging the Atocha's sister ship, Santa Margarita. We'll visit her remains in a future message. I spent the 1986 diving season helping extract her riches.

It was common sense and custom to anchor our boats on the lee side of the Marquesas for safe shelter. Never did we risk the possibility of sudden storms and their inherent winds and waves on the open ocean at night. Atocha was left to slumber again nightly. By sunset we'd be at our safe anchorage whether we had dove on the galleon that day or arrived late on the first day. "Two post" was the nickname of the anchorage off of the skull-shaped Marquesas. Yup, skull-shaped, Sam. **You,** couldn't have written it better. The souls and treasure of the two galleons had lain there over three centuries off of the shore of Skull Island before Mel claimed and freed them.

An evening and night at the "two post anchorage" was remarkable. After securing the anchor to the sandy bottom and turning off the engines, a quiet swept over the decks. To go from the rumbling of twin diesels and their vibrations to swinging gently on the bow anchor off the shore of the beloved island was a change, indeed. The fresh ocean breeze replaced the smell of fumes. The perception of it all was akin to stepping back in time. On top of this marine sublimity, I felt the anticipation of what might happen the next day. The **Atocha** beckoned a few miles from our anchorage. "Today's the Day!" Well, tomorrow was at least.

As you can imagine, the tranquility didn't last for long with a crew of men in their prime living out their dream. Some of the divers had various weapons on board consisting of pistols, shotguns, M-16's and A-K 47's. An impromptu firing-line at the gunnel made for an exciting display of reports filling the once fresh ocean air with the smell of spent gunpowder as we blasted away at debris of every sort floating past us in the current at different speeds and distances. The entire scene was as much for show as well as sport. The sounds of gunfire traveled miles over the open water forewarning any pirates our operation was not easy-pickings should they be entertaining thoughts of attacking and taking the valuable fruits of our labor. News of the discovery of the "golden galleon" had gone worldwide. We were almost thirty miles from any assistance. Even at sea we had to be able to put up a fight until the cavalry arrived. Divers were fired upon a few years earlier by a rogue craft but no one was wounded. Our defense system was not one of paranoia.

Another order of business was supper. A cook was rarely provided as one of the crew. We rotated the duty. The rule was... if you cooked, you didn't do cleanup, and vice versa. Every couple days, depending on crew size, the responsibility of one of the chores became yours. Given a choice, I liked cooking the best. Our culinary talents varied by some degree, but not much. The chow ranged from good to excellent. The small propane stove/oven in the galley was used to it's fullest capabilities. For a few months we had an official cook aboard the **Virgalona**. One expedition was during Thanksgiving. Wonderful smells drifted out of the galley all day and the cook kept us warded-off for secrecy. She surprised us with a definitive dinner complete with baked turkey. My cooking skills have been of high quality since the time of my youth. One of my first jobs was as fry cook and dishwasher at an all night truck stop in Leadington, Missouri. The crew of our boat always complimented my efforts. Mel made sure we were well stocked with such a variety of foodstuffs. An army runs on it's stomach. After dinner when every minor chore was completed, such as, checking the condition of the bilge pumps, the crew engaged in bullshitting on the deck. Us newbies, if we were smart,

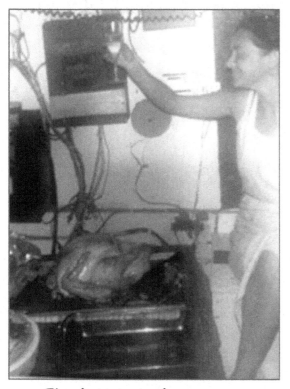

Thanksgiving turkey
with Genevieve Lear

kept our mouths mostly shut as veteran crew members, as well as the captain, spun stories of past discoveries and experiences during the search for Atocha. One by one we'd drop out of the gathering to make our way to our bunks.

Every morning we'd arise before the sun and be on site as soon as possible. Sack time was reading time for most of us. Rarely has anything ever brought me as much comfort as tucking myself into the bleach smelling bedding while I read a good book and listened to the sea lapping on the hull. The sound made my eyes slowly blink shut with my latest read resting on my chest. In that aquatic cradle, I always slept well. Oddly, in spite of the circumstance of my repose, I never dreamed of finding treasure. I think those dreams were spent during waking hours. There were no treasure dreams left to wish for. They'd arrived and we were poised to live them. We were living them.

Sam, in... **"Three Thousand Years Against The Microbes"**, you wrote about dreams. You said..."A dream that comes only once is oftenest only an idle accident, and hasn't any message, but the recurrent dream is quite another matter-oftener than not it has come on business". I'm fortunate your view also applied to daydreaming.

I'm off to bed, Sam. Goodnight. In the next message we'll be at the wreck-site withdrawing treasure from, "The Bank Of Spain". HA!

Hambone

Message Thirty-four...
"Sun, Salt and Salving"
January 29, 2015
Cape Girardeau, Mo.

Dear Sam,

Mornings at "two post anchorage" came early. Before the sun was peeking above the horizon, the boat came alive with the crew swilling coffee and maybe having a smoke. We scrounged the galley for some breakfast and the energy it provided until lunch. After the meal and some preps we were alerted by the start of the engines to get off our duffs and prepare to start a strenuous action packed day lasting until sunset. After the diesels were warmed-up, half the crew would report to the bow of **Virgalona** to pull the anchor imbedded in the sea bottom. Without the benefit of a hydraulic winch for the task, it took three of us to pull in a few hundred feet of anchor line, coil it perfectly and bring the heavy anchor aboard under the watchful eye of the captain as he steered toward the anchor's location. Once the hook was aboard and lashed down securely we headed for the site. It was a good twenty minute run. Without an order given, the crew prepared itself for arrival at our selected coordinates and setting up the boat for our first excavation of the morning.

Upon arrival we threw a reference buoy on Atocha's remains, attached to a line and cinderblock on where we believed "**X**" marked the spot. Just as Mike and I would do nine years into the future on that harrowing Ides of March, we would proceed into the wind away from the buoy some distance, throw the bow anchor for a firm hold and back-down the salvage boat until the buoy appeared off the stern. At this point one of us would pull alongside

151

the stern in a small Boston Whaler boat we towed along with us. We handed the diver the stern anchor of **Virgalona** which was attached to hundreds of feet of stout line. Off they went skipping the anchor behind the Whaler as they kept an eye on the captain's hand signals indicating which direction to go, and...when to drop the anchor and set it. After throwing the anchor at the required distance, those of us on deck would pull in the line to set it tightly into the bottom. On occasion, the anchor wouldn't set

Ham with a cinderblock

firmly. In that case, the diver running the support boat would have to jump overboard in his already donned scuba gear, find the troublesome anchor and secure it in the seafloor by hand. It was a hazardous maneuver. Chasing a wayward anchor across the bottom with assorted lines attached to it, then capturing it's stock like the horns of a pissed-off bull is not easy...but we did it. After capturing the anchor, we had to jam it's flukes into the bottom and hope it's forward motion eased the task of acquiring a firm hold. It usually did... sometimes not. The entire process was repeated with the other stern anchor. Prepping the boat for operations on site consumed an hour on a good day. With the bow and stern anchors deployed, we were held fast on a web of three anchor lines. That condition was required in order for us to do our work.

152

Captain R.D. LeClaire at Virgalona's helm.

The boat had to be firmly held in place directly over the target we sought beneath the block holding the buoy in place.

Next, came the lowering of the "mail boxes" which were invented by Mel. These devices weighed hundreds of pounds apiece and were constructed of steel or aluminum. They are "L-shaped" hollow tubes that are mounted on the stern. When released, they pivoted ninety degrees and swung into position over the propellors of the Virgalona. One of us would fasten the device into place under the boat with steel pins. As the sea rocked the boat the huge tubes would swing freely causing difficulty until they were secured. At the completion of that task, it was always great to come up from under the boat with all fingers accounted for and noggin intact.

With the boat held in place and the mailboxes ready to excavate a crater on the sea floor, the captain engaged the transmission putting the propellors in motion and slowly increased their power to the proper r.p.m.'s. Depending on the depth of the dive, we generally took twenty to thirty minutes to blow a hole. The blue water behind the boat turned the color of the sea bottom we were churning up. Virgalona strained against the anchor lines that held her fast. We kept a wary eye on the anchors and

Captain R.D. LeClaire directing drop-anchor

the bite they held. All too often they would dislodge from where they bit. When that happened, all digging ceased as a diver labored to secure them once again. The boat vibrated immensely during a dig. We shook from head to toe from the effects of it with the anticipation of leaving the surface to swim down into the hole to detect for and claim riches, whether they be intrinsic or valuable historic data...usually both.

Hambone

Message Thirty-five...
"Searching the Deep"
February 2, 2015
Cape Girardeau, Mo.

Dear Sam,

Damn it's a cold and windy day! At least I don't feel an obligation to be outside working or recreating. I do look forward to doing some metal detecting locally. But today is a day for tending to matters indoors. It's a good day to write you.

So, back to the Atocha site and our efforts to find treasure. After the blow-hole was complete and ready to be examined, the first two divers in the rotation went over the side, did a surface gear check, then disappeared as they finned down to the sixty foot depth. Each frogman carried a metal detector and a mesh bag containing various implements needed for the task at hand. The divers remaining behind tended to various jobs such as filling scuba tanks or whatever was deemed necessary to the operation. Everyone kept a watchful eye for sharks or any peril that could endanger a diver on the open ocean. We tracked divers' positions on the bottom by watching their bubbles breaking the surface.

After a good look at the newly excavated hole for obvious finds, we prepped for a thorough search of it. When doing a circle search, we clipped onto the line tied to our buoy floating on the surface. The line varied in length depending on the width of the crater. While unspooling the line, we went to the outermost edge of the hole, pulled the line tight and swam the circumference of the hole while metal detecting and visually searching. After one orbit of the hole we moved a meter toward the center the hole and swam the circumference again and again until we covered the

155

area of the entire dig. Before surfacing, the outside of the hole was checked visually for obvious wreckage and anything that may have been ejected by the vortex water-column from the mailboxes.

Sam, there's a hell of a lot more trash in the ocean than treasure...so, much of our time on the bottom was spent digging-up metal objects of every sort including bombs dropped by our country's warbirds. Not far from Atocha's grave lay the fragments of the target ship Patricia. Errant ordinance dropped on her littered the twelve mile swath of the scatter pattern of Atocha. Just like when I dig worthless junk in Hannibal, it's time consuming and frustrating to put out the effort for say...a rusty beer can when you're expecting treasure. Luckily, the bombs were inert but I still puckered during an excavation of one. Like all the other metallic junk we found, we raised it to the surface. It made no sense to leave it in place risking rediscovering it again with a magnetometer or another sensing device wasting time diving on it yet...again! Judging from the remains of the Patricia, real bombs were dropped on her. Some major chunks of her were surrounded by deformed steel

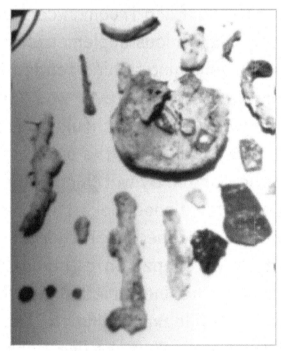

Pewter plate / coins / pottery shards
fasteners from Margarita

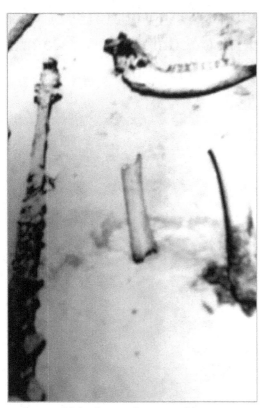

Sword blade and animal bones
from Margarita

beams and thousands of fragments of her blasted remains. On occasion, the warrior airmen would buzz our boats at close low altitude and speed. Their afterburners rocked our ears and boats. It was exhilarating. We swore they were using us as a practice-run for strafing the Patricia. I remember an account of bullets from one of the fighters jets coming close to one of the salvage boats. A pilot had mistaken one of Mel's boats, the Arbutus, for the target ship.

More than our share of dives ended up with the discovery of Spanish loot, especially during the first months of the discovery of Atocha. With our boats anchored over her, it was a veritable treasure factory in a sense. The rescue of tons of silver, hundreds of thousands of coins and every artifact representing what the doomed passengers and crew needed for the long voyage to Spain, kept us busy surfacing with the latest find to be admired and awed at. We weren't simply latching onto and swimming to the surface with these new finds. Before removal, the location of each one was recorded for the site map. We performed sound archaeology on Atocha, Sam, I carry-on with the standard to this day with the Amy Elizabeth Cape wreck and your turf in Hannibal.

More on the **Atocha** and her sister ship, **Margarita**, later. I have more errands and chores to attend to. Goodnight Mr. Twain....
Hambone

Pieces of Atocha Eights...my first finds.
Photo: the crew

Dear Sam,

I'm struggling with where to go next. Do we stay at the treasure site and dig up some bounty? Or...leave the motherlode and return to Hannibal to tender stories left untold waiting in the wings? The **Amy Elizabeth** wreck is producing more information here at the Cape that warrants sharing with you, and...we will return to Atocha many times when we talk. Staying with one subject for too long might bore you. Having no clue about writing compels me to take due caution by switching our location among these historic sites and their known revelations. Let's update all three.

Spring is springing relatively soon. With the accompanying weather, my mind will be occupied by more thoughts of Hannibal for the first search of 2015. The expectation of immediately finding artifacts is not far fetched. They are a reality. Rarely can a treasure hunter flat-out state he will find artifacts in the next hole. I'm not merely saying it...I'm shouting it! The hole I found the assortment of artifacts in last year is where I'll commence. I know there's more objects to be uncovered in that area. In the downpour of rain last year I rescued the assortment of glass, coal and other remnants that qualified it as a honey hole.

My method will be deliberate and without haste. This refuse pile is broader than the hole I bored into it after finding it with my trusty detector and pin-pointer last season. After relocating the spot, I will grid it into a three by three foot square using stakes and string as it's boundaries. Using my trowel and any tools necessary, I will roll back the green turf covering the spot. It's essential to be able to replace the turf when I leave to avoid blemishing the fine grass carpet surrounding your boyhood home. At that point I will wave my pin-pointer over the exposed area and mark with stakes any metallic hits it indicates. The slow process of removing dirt will be performed by stripping away even layers around 1/4" thick. As the dig continues, artifacts encountered will be photographed in-situ, triangulated and removed carefully. I'm looking forward to the next Hannibal expedition, to say the least.

The Cape Girardeau wreck is still submerged, Sam. I haven't returned to it since last month when I found the vintage ink bottle protruding from the riverbank. Although I'm positive of finding artifacts immediately while I'm in Hannibal, next time...I can't be as optimistic about immediate results on **Amy Elizabeth.** After the river drops, giving me access to the foundered ship and her batteries for extraction and examination, I hope to know more of the age and history of her. It would be most fortunate if the Mississippi falls to the required eight foot level during a spell of warm weather. I have controlled optimism of a great revelation about the boat this year. Although the craft was silted over to the levels of 2013 when I last saw her, I believe the river will again expose her enough to allow an agreeable level of observable detail. The muck covering her was frozen in place causing it to cling to the wreckage, resisting the erosive effects of waves kicked up by passing towboats.

The Cape Girardeau River Heritage Museum has expressed an interest in displaying photos and information about the wreck. I delivered them a sample of the images I have on hand for their consideration. The wreck is an important part of our local river heritage even with the incomplete knowledge of it. I haven't heard back from them. They're closed until mid March and are preparing exhibits for the coming season. Perhaps I'll hear from them soon. If I don't, I'll contact them and lobby for the exhibition. Unfortunately, I can't provide pieces from the wreck for display. Until a qualified archaeologist is willing to excavate the wreck, nothing can be removed legally, as you well know from previous

Cape River Heritage Museum

messages. What is there...remains there, to be either preserved by the river, washed away or removed by thieves. Laws protecting her have doomed her so far. The original decking is gone. Exposure to air and sunlight corrodes her. Vandals, while their acts have been minimal, have removed a few objects and disfigured a portion of her.

Work continues on the Atocha site. Any day we could hear of the discovery of her golden stern-castle, the object of the search at hand. Debs and I are heading to Key West to join in the celebration of the thirtieth anniversary of her discovery on July 20th.....   Hambone

Dear Sam,

Happy Valentine's Day! To mark the occasion, Debs and I took her parents to a catfish lunch yesterday. We dined at The Port Cape Restaurant next to the Mississippi River. I trust that Olivia, you and the girls expressed your love to each other today. The love between family members is non-extinguishable and eternal, whether in another place unknown to us mortals, or in our daily lives.

Almost a week has passed since I started this message. It's now the 19th of February. A winter storm dumped a foot of snow on our region and beyond. My days have been spent shoveling the driveway and important paths so we'd not be shut-ins. Last night a couple inches of freezing rain and sleet topped off the abundant snowbanks. After a week of sub freezing temperatures the mercury hovers around 38 degrees today. Last night's ice that clung to the tallest trees is falling on the property. Shards of frozen projectiles, including damaged limbs, are making a trip to the mailbox a hazardous one. In spite of a ten day bout of cabin fever, Debs hasn't thumped cur Barney or me. Her patience is remarkable as my furry partner and I wander between my office upstairs and the shop/man-cave in the basement making messes of every sort. Life goes on until the respite of spring, which will usher in total industry for me of many sorts. Before I know it, I'll be busy with swimming pool maintenance and digging in the dirt for secrets to be unlocked...whether in Hannibal, **Amy Elizabeth,** or other sites that await my attention. The affliction of cabin fever is at an intolerable level for me. I fear the remainder of winter is going to put me over the edge.

As I reread the previous paragraph, it reminded me of something you said..."It's spring fever. That is what the name of it is. And when you've got it, you want...oh, you don't quite know what it is you want, but it just fairly makes your heart ache, you want it so!" Sam, I reckon I have the fever for sure. I'm going to assume and go with that. At least I'm assured by your words my condition is not permanent...that the affliction of my mind and body will be soothed in the coming month of March by the rebirth of the barren, cold landscape into greenery and the flora and fauna that dwell within it...

Hambone

Dear Sam,

The eerie task we were performing on a dark early morning near Landau, Germany seemed grimmer as a Deutch fog shrouded the compound. The floodlights illuminating the area were diffused but made it possible for us to prepare the missiles for launch. It was 1976, Sam. The cold war was alive and well. As we came out of our own personal...just awoken fog, we entered another one as we labored under the watchful eyes of the company commander and his officers. We were unable to detect by their stance or actions if what we were doing was another drill, or the first salvo's of World War III. Half of the Nike-Hercules missiles were tipped with W-31 20 kilo-ton nuclear warheads. The remaining ballistic rockets carried conventional high explosives.

Nike-Hercules launch
Photo: U.S. Army

The W-31 Nuclear warheads packed the explosive power of the bombs dropped on Hiroshima and Nagasaki. As the citizens of Landau slept, they were unaware of the frenzy of activity that consumed our attention. No sirens wailed any sort of audible alert. Only the most attentive outsider would have noticed the increased

164

illumination around the missile barns that secured these javelins of Armageddon. Each missile was mounted on a track. With controlled haste, four of us carefully pushed one missile at a time horizontally down the rail until it latched into it's launcher. A technical team fastened various cable connectors in place and made final checks of the beasts as they were being prepared to be raised to the desired angle for launch.

After the missiles were deemed ready for firing, each one was raised toward the dark and starry European sky by a missile-man throwing a switch in the blast proof concrete and earthen bunker. It was surreal. It was pulse quickening. The hydraulic motors whined a high-shrilled banshee-noise as they lifted tons of explosives and missile components slowly upward. A fitting noise it was considering what we were about to possibly do. Like erect and ready soldiers, the missiles hovered over us in launch position. Then, they seemed to come alive as their control surfaces snapped back and forth with a humming and whirring audible click. Before entering the bunker, the last task we did was the closing of the storage barn doors. This was to prevent any damage to the inside of the structure should we actually launch. As we heaved on the thick gauge chains controlling the opening and closing of the doors, someone usually joked, if we did launch these warbirds...who gives a rat's ass if the inside of the barn is damaged or not? Who would possibly be left to even care! Oh well...we still closed them as due in regulations...the, "Army way".

For the final countdown we hurried-to and huddled-in the protective bunker. The confines of the bunker were intimate, to say the least. The ventilation barely provided ample air for the crowded control room. We were packed in there with the team of technicians, missile-men and us...the Military Policemen. Our vigil could last for minutes or hours. As "small talk" took place, we kept notice of a red light on the control panel that indicated the first missile was armed and ready to fly. If it turned green, it was the order to fire. Although it was unspoken, it was known that if the order to fire was received, it had to be followed through. It could be up to us M. P.'s to enforce the firing order even if it took the threat of, or the use of...deadly force. What madness the situation was! These men were our friends and comrades. We stood by in our blast-proof shelter and waited in an atmosphere of sweat, pride, hope and fear.....our Nike-Hercules weapons system's range was considerable and it's power infinite.

The hellish weapons poised to leave the launchpad were two staged and used solid propellant. Their length was almost forty feet and had a wingspan of six feet. Each missile weighed over five tons and maxed-out in speed at a little over Mach 3.5 or 2,688 mph! Their range was 95 miles. The Nike-Herc's were developed to counter the threat of Soviet bomber squadrons, should the "Commie bastardos" attack the west. Just one of the 20 kiloton warheads detonated near scores of planes would have been most effective. The Nike-Herc system used it's two minute flight time efficiently. The missiles could be rigged for surface to surface attack. Also...Sam, I had to share this with you to continue our journey. There is a connection to you that made it necessary to drag you to what was then, West Germany near the French border. I'll fill you in with the next message. Home duty calls...

Hambone

Message Thirty-nine...
"Thomas Nast"
March 29, 2015
Cape Girardeau, Mo.

Dear Sam,

It's been almost a month since I've written. I had the misfortune of having emergency gallbladder surgery! Damn the luck. The operation itself was relatively easy and quick. After two days in the hospital I was released and found myself returning to the emergency room four hours later with an inoperable bladder. After a week of wearing a urine bag strapped to my leg and a catheter poked up me, I'm back to normal. I had plenty of time to write during my recovery but the mood wasn't there. I'm glad to be back in touch with you as I pound away on my keyboard on a much anticipated spring day. I'm not even sure where I left off in Message 38. Pardon me while I read it again.

Oh yeah...we left off in Landau, Germany preparing nuclear missiles for a launch that never happened. The event was well practiced and duty was served. Hopefully, I conveyed to you the harsh reality of what we felt as we worked through what we prayed was a war-game and nothing beyond. They say there are no atheists in a foxhole. I can say there are no atheists in a protective bunker anticipating the changing of a firing light from red to green, possibly bringing about the extinction of civilization as we know it. Had we released our lightning on Soviet bombers, nuclear retaliation by the Russians would've been certain.

Whatever the political scenario was that would've led to our launching drill becoming a reality, wouldn't have mattered to us. We would simply have had to launch! Politicians seeking a victory would give the order. We were to pull the trigger. While we would've had blood on our hands, they would've had blood on their souls. Which wound would have been worse? Thank God, I didn't find out. Your words in **"Mark Twain...A Biography"** define duty as... "A man's first duty is to his own conscience and honor; the party and country come second to that, and never first." That wasn't the case at B/256 Army Defense Artillery. We **would** have launched.

Thirty five years before this stressful missile drill, Mel Fisher advanced across Germany as a young officer in the Engineer Corp. World War II wrenched him and hundreds of thousands of our nation's finest to quell another war with the Germans. Mel's duty was to build bridges, POW camps and whatever else deemed important to the cause. Mel was wounded by a sniper in the neck and suffered vision problems for the rest of his life because of the injury. Mel once used the labor of two hundred German POW'S to build their own prison camp!

Our mission at B/256 Air Defense Artillery was to keep the peace and fill the power vacuum created by the defeat of the Germans by Mel and the Allied Armies. Although it was called the cold war, the white hot nuclear flashpoint loomed for several decades. I can attest that the nukes would have been launched if the order came down. What if we had launched? The collateral damage to innocent lives and property would have paled the holocaust. Our excuse would have been... "We were merely following orders." That sounds familiar. I cannot fathom how Hitler and his generals gave orders for the defenseless death of genocide. However, I can understand why it was carried out by dutiful soldiers, blind to their own conscious and honor, steered by perceived duty and twisted justification, whether it be duty or fear of joining their victims in a firing squad.

The barracks we lived in overlooked the missile compound and the city of Landau. We were referred to by the Landau citizenry as... "the Americans on the hill." The proper name of our base was, Camp Thomas Nast. Although I was at Camp Nast for a year, I never knew it's official military moniker. We simply called our quartering area as "up-range" and we referred to the missile area as "down-range". It's amazing what can evade you when you're young and foolish, and foolish we were in spite of the horrendous power and responsibility we shouldered keeping the peace by threatening "all out destruction" in post World War II Germany.

Thomas Nast was born in the barracks of Landau on September 27, 1840 and emigrated to New York City with his family in 1846. Early in his life he showed an interest and skill as an illustrator. In 1859, he gained attention from, **"Harper's Weekly"**. **"Harpers"** published drawings of Nast's to illustrate a report on police corruption. Nast's popularity surged and captured America's imagination with his overseas coverage with illustrations and stories of the Garibaldi military campaign to unify Italy. On the home-front, he rose to the Union cause during the Civil War by illustrating southern and border state battlefields. His cartoon, **"Compromise with the South"**, was widely accepted and celebrated. The illustration depicted the Northerners who were against fighting the rebel states. Abraham Lincoln referred to your old friend Nast as, "Our best recruiting Sergeant".

While Thomas battled social injustice through illustrated medium and powerful cutlines, you, Sam, also identified the injustices inflicted on man with a river of ink that evoked illustrations through the theatre of our minds. Both of you had a big dog in the fight for the little guy simply trying to maintain an earned life against corruption, both government and public imposed. The letters exchanged between Nast and yourself are fascinating and reveal a deep respect between you and Thomas.

On an empty hillside overlooking Landau, Germany, is the former site of our barracks compound. Camp Thomas Nast is no more. It was bulldozed and removed in the late 1980's. The Nike-Herc missiles are gone. The launch site of those nuclear arrows was replaced by a battery of Patriot missiles. The Patriot system, despite being non-nuclear, is an effective means of defense against missiles and aircraft. The nuclear fire was never released from Landau.

Camp Thomas Nast existed for over thirty years. Although the duty was grueling during my time there, I look back fondly at that chapter of my life. Thousands of us missile guardians, and missile-men passed through it's mission. What we participated in was necessary. Had we been forced to launch, it would have been catastrophic to all civilization. We were boys, Sam...just boys.

Hambone

Dear Sam,

I can't fathom seven months passing since I wrote you last. So much has happened since March. I have plenty to tell you about during the coming "cabin fever" Winter. It's not difficult to pick a starting point for the flood of letters to come. Two weeks ago I was back in Hannibal digging after a one year hiatus. The discoveries I made are amazing, Sam! It was the best expedition to Hannibal yet.

For almost a year to the day I'd been trying to get back to Hannibal to resume where I left off...the spot in your yard which produced an assortment of items convincing me I'd stumbled across a refuse pile or privy. A year is a long time to wait when a mystery awaits further investigation. The artifacts on my workbench in the shop have been a daily reminder of anticipated discoveries. I expected to be in Hannibal town no later than July.

After one cancelled trip, I finally made it back to Hannibal a few weeks ago. The weather forecast was excellent for digging. It was either, go for it, or take a chance of it being the last window of opportunity to search before the rains and the unstable weather of Fall are on the horizon. The forecast called for seventy degrees and mostly sunny skies. I knew Hannibal had experienced a bout with rain which promised the soil wouldn't have the hardness of concrete, yet not so messy my electronic gear would not be thrown off by excess moisture. Although I had several swimming pools left to tend to after the exhausting season, I consolidated them into a one day a week effort. Weather, time and the demands of life lined up perfectly.

Road weary from the drive, I rolled across Bear Creek bridge on the outskirts of Hannibal. The forecast was holding and the weather was sunny and warm. Excitement electrified the air as I checked into my regular lodging a stones throw from your boyhood home at 208 Hill Street. Since my travel went smoothly from Cape to Hannibal, there was still enough daylight left to make preparations for digging on the artifact-rich location...the same place I was forced to abandon during my last visit when I ran out of time and struggled in the rainy, lightning-laced conditions.

In order to stretch my legs a bit, I left the hotel with my equipment and walked to your boyhood home first. I checked in with the various tour guides and shopkeepers so they'd be aware of my presence and purpose for the next few days. No one has clearance to metal detect and dig on the properties except me. I didn't want to be mistaken for a trespasser. I'm glad I did check in...the employees I greeted were all new to me. I returned to the spot of my greatest interest and took a look. Any concern that I may have blemished the fine yard from my previous work was quickly squashed. Not a blemish or dimple was evident from my previous efforts. I sat at the concrete table and bench next to the stone wall and carefully laid out all my digging, recording and detecting devices. All the items were accounted for.

With tape measure, string and wooden stakes in hand I approached last year's artifact laden honey-hole. I knew the exact location of it. The triangulated coordinates were in my field notes from the previous year. As I extended the tape measure from the iron gate in the wall, I thought of my old comrade, Mike

Fulmer. The buried plaque I found two years earlier came off the gate. He has been gone nearly five years.

Grid one refuse area.

Reminiscing of Mike caused me to think of Mel. I muttered, "Today's the day!", as I started setting up a grid with the string and wooden stakes on the measurement where "**X**" hopefully marked the spot of my previous fruitful dig. Starting with a one by one foot hole seemed desirable. It would allow me to burrow a core-sample deep and make recordation of any artifacts in-situ easier to triangulate and photograph.

I fetched my metal-detector off the table and turned it on. It came to life flashing light and sound. As I swept it's energized search-coil over the grid I'd roped off, no sound came from the detector. It was no surprise not getting a hit. Keep in mind, the area of my interest was discovered as a result of a scrap of iron the previous October. The rest of the haul was composed of glass, coal, crock-ware and ceramic fragments of cups. Before digging, I tested both of my detectors in the side garden as well as my pin-pointer. I detected and passed over and around ten metallic targets under the soil. It was tempting to pause and dig, having waited a year for the opportunity. I kept to my plan and returned my attention back to the prepared spot.

As planned, I traced the hole with my sharp blade to loosen the edge of the grass. Slipping the edge of the trowel beneath the sod and working inward allowed me to prepare the grass for rolling it back. It worked pretty well, not perfect...but well enough to open a window to the past. I placed the square of topsoil on a towel to protect and preserve it. Faced with an exposed grassless square area, I sat back and contemplated continuing or "packing it in" until early the next morning. The shadows in the courtyard were growing longer and my belly was growling. All things considered, I merely probed the exposed dirt with a long screwdriver to a depth of around eight inches. Excitement abounded as I felt resistance to the probe as I pushed it in carefully at different spots, knowing full well the items resisting the probe could be rocks and roots. I contained my excitement until the actual excavating proved otherwise. I placed a sheet of plastic over the spot and lugged my equipment back to my lodging up the hill. Once I stored the gear, I retrieved my bicycle from the back of my van and pedaled to downtown Hannibal in search of the greasiest cheeseburger possible and a beer.

Sam..as I sat at an outdoor table enjoying my supper and drink, I took-in the ambience of the street you walked and played on. After a second beer, I hopped back on the bike and headed to my room to turn in early after a swim and spa time. The bed was comfortable and much needed. I read for awhile and dozed off with the book on my chest. My alarm was set for six a.m. The forecast was holding. I was set. Tomorrow is going to be THE day... I hoped...

Hambone

Dear Sam,

In one of your notebooks you wrote about expectations. You said..."A thing long expected takes the form of the unexpected when at last it comes". As I lugged my digging gear to your boyhood home, I allowed myself the rare opportunity of allowing myself high expectations in the hole I'd carefully prepped the evening before.

Much to my alarm the grounds were soaked when I got there! The sprinklers had kicked-on in the wee hours and did their duty of refreshing the parched lawn and plants. It didn't cross my pea-brained mind to shut the water off the evening before. With my heart pounding and a few whispered expletives of frustration, I approached the plastic covered grid. I yanked the covering off hoping water hadn't slipped underneath it. Relief replaced my annoyance. My grid was dry! The plastic had protected it from a good soaking by the sprinklers.

When I yanked the plastic off, some of the stakes became dislodged and the string marking the grid was in disarray. It was a quick chore to fix it all. I put an empty bucket next to the grid to serve as a receptacle for loose and screened dirt. Next to it I spread out a towel to serve as a resting place for artifacts freshly dug. High expectations abounded. It is rare that a treasure hunter or archaeologist can enjoy guaranteed success before one trowel of earth has been turned. This was one of those moments. To walk away at the end of this day without a fantastic discovery didn't seem ponderable. The discovery of artifacts near my grid the previous October and good ole intuition fueled it all. On my hands and knees I positioned myself to begin the process of scraping away layers of earth and time. It didn't take long before my back and knees ached. I didn't care. "Today's the day!"..........Hambone

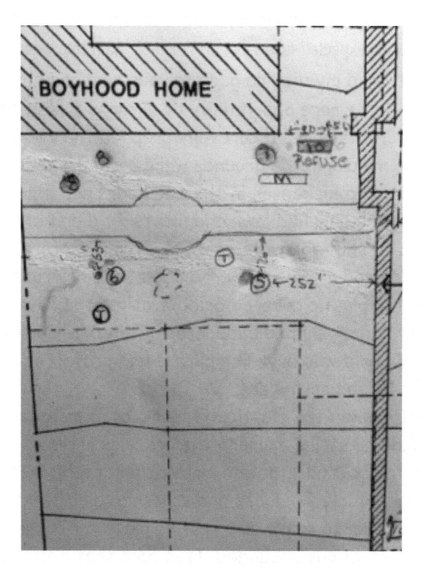

Location of refuse pit in relation with
boyhood home.

Message Forty-two...
"One Man's Trash"
January 22, 2016
Cape Girardeau, Mo.

Dear Sam,

"Today's the day!", it was! Before I penetrated the soil by a mere few inches, I encountered layer upon layer of artifacts confirming the last dig of 2015 was indeed a refuse area. So much material appeared, I had to contain my excitement and slow down. Good archaeology doesn't mean wrenching items from the ground in haste to see what's going to be discovered next. For the next few days I focused on the spot in a methodical and controlled manner.

Realizing it truly **was** a "dump area", or possibly the remnants of a privy, I decided to narrow the width of the hole. By doing so,

One of two test holes.

it allowed me to go deeper, quicker...and in doing so, I would produce sound field-work. I excavated two holes during the three day effort. I dug each one to the depth of how far my hand and trowel could reach into each hole while laying on my stomach, or basically three feet. Volume-wise, I estimated all of the newly found traces of the past were removed from an area of mere one cubic foot of dirt. Just as in 2015, the spot

177

produced fragments of glass, broken ceramic, coal, pieces of bricks, bones, fasteners and bits of chinaware. Much to my surprise, an intact sugar bowl top appeared.

Next, was a complete handle off of a glass stein. A long lost clay gaming marble, perhaps surrendered by a circle of boys participating in a frenzied game, was mixed with the other articles from long ago. It initially looked like a musket-ball until I wiped away the dirt from it and used my pin-pointer, verifying it's composition to be organic and non metallic.

One frustration that comes with the job of digging-up artifacts is the lack of identifying marks on objects discovered. Besides the red lettered quarters that spelled-out, D-A-Y on my first expedition, nothing I'd dug up was identified by characters. That dry spell is over now. I found items with maker's marks. The first one with the name of the maker was a beautiful intact clear glass medicine bottle with an "H" stamped on the bottom. I traced the bottle to the W.H. Hamilton & Company, circa 1898-1918, Pittsburg, Pennsylvania. It's a fine bottle, Sam. Not a chip mars it's semi-iridescent body. While a few other bottle makers have also used the, "H", mark...the preponderance of evidence points to Hamilton. Deeper into the excavation I found a

Hamilton bottle;
American Glass Works

broken bottle base. Stamped on the bottom was a circled "A". I traced this bottle to The American Glassworks 1908-1935, Richmond Virginia and Paden City, West Virginia. American Glassworks ceased using the mark 1910-1911, The Armstrong Cork Company also used the Circle "A" trademark from 1939-1969, years after registering the mark in April, 1889. How American Glasswork was also able to use the mark is unknown to me. A piece of glazed pottery that appears to be the bottom of a saucer or cup was recovered. It was stamped, TRADE MARK PREMIUM GRANITE B.B.M.& Co. Pictured above the script is a deer's head with a fine rack of a dozen points. B.B.M. & Co. stood for, The Brunt, Bloor, Martin and Company 1875-1882, Staffordshire-East Liverpool Pottery District.

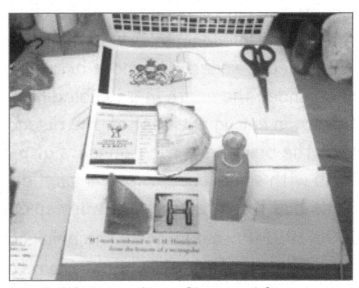

S.P.C.O. Iron Stone China; and Company artifacts being tagged and researched at home.

179

Shards of cups, saucers and glass before tagging.

Another piece of marked ceramic from an object unknown is stamped in a crowned-shield featuring two lions appearing to be holding it up from opposite sides. Written on the shield is, S.P.C.O. IRON STONE CHINA. It came from the Sebring Pottery Company, founded by Frank Sebring in 1887 at East Liverpool, Ohio. Around 1898 the works moved to Sebring, Ohio.

I encountered a lot of large brick fragments during the three day effort. Some were nearly whole bricks. Most of them were half and quarter pieces. When I began discovering them in number, it caused me to wonder if I truly was digging the old privy and if the bricks were lining the wall of it's subterranean chamber as was the custom with that day and time. That theory waned. The more brick I found proved them to be piled under the earth in a jumbled manner. Obviously they were thrown in among the rest of the discarded things. It is plausible that the bricks are the remnants of a chimney that collapsed in 1885 with such force, the rear portion of the second floor of the home had to be removed. It was replaced during a restoration in 1990-1991. Examination of the bricks does show a black discoloration you would expect from the inner bricks of a chimney. Whatever it was that destroyed the bricks, it wrecked them all at once. They were discarded together fresh from the same trauma.

It was easier to throw them into the refuse pit than haul them to the river. I do hope the brick are from the collapsed chimney. I reburied most of the brick pieces and saved a few for closer examination. Hopefully, this means the refuse pile goes back to at least 1884. There is a possibility this honey-hole goes back to your time at the home, Sam...1844-1853.

Several pieces of the ceramic shards had floral patterns on them of different designs. A few coffee or tea cup pieces had gold banding around the top. They looked expensive and out of place. I imagine whoever broke them wasn't thrilled at the time. I'm able to jigsaw a few of those remnants together. I lack too many other pieces to succeed in forming them into a complete cup. Besides pieces of brick and coal, the last artifact I released from the soil was the torso of a figurine or doll made of china. It measures 3" by 2". It was a fun find. Of all the hundred or so items pulled from your yard, I believe this to be the only example of an object of non utility. Everything up until now have been objects that served a purpose of construction, sustenance, living shelter, warmth and survival. The headless torso was both aesthetic and playful. It wasn't needed for survival.

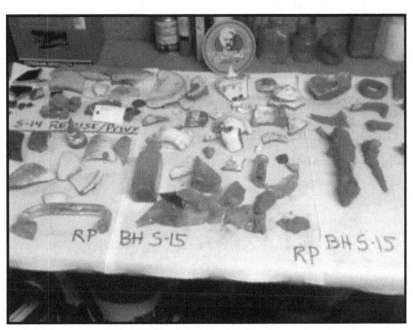

The collection is growing.

It graced a table or was the remnants of some little Hannibal girl's, "Dolly".

It's time to hit the hay, Sam. I'll pick it back up in message forty three....

Hambone

Happy treasure finder!
Photo: Debra Barnhouse

Dear Sam,

Needless to say, I was more than pleased with the results of my one and only effort in Hannibal in 2015, especially having recovered so much material and soooo much more left in the ground for 2016 attempts. That's right, Mr. Clemens...when I abandoned my efforts and left for home, I was still recovering artifacts. Almost every scrape of my trowel revealed bits and pieces of material. Every scoop of dirt dumped and investigated was a thrill. It made me think of the Atocha salvage days in '85. That great galleon's resting place was a depository of not only treasure but thousands of shards of pottery in great number. The pulverized ceramic bits on the sea floor surrounding and mixing in with her broken remains were the remnants of storage vessels containing stores for delivery and victuals for the voyage to Spain.

What is it that never leaves us satisfied and buoyed in spirit soon after a more than satisfactory experience? As I toted my gear and spoils of my effort to the van, I was already feeling some deflation of my spirit as I exited the grounds. I felt great considering the breakthrough made with the refuse area. At the same time, I was certain none of the discoveries could be attributed to your era at the home. I knew it would be months, maybe even a year before I could return to dig deeper and wider. My bags were chock full of goodies, perhaps a doubling of the amount of the entire collection, yet...they were void of anything belonging to you or your family.

On the way back to Cape Girardeau I detoured down U.S. Highway 67 and swung through St. Francois County to visit with family. I met with niece Stacey, sister Brenda and nephew Danny. As we visited I unpacked the dirty, crusty finds for them to see and hold. I'm fairly sure they were interested to the level they conveyed, maybe part of it was just humoring their crazy relative as I babbled and revealed my treasures. Time passed too quickly with my loved ones. Before I knew it, I was traveling east on Route 32 to Interstate 55 for the hour and a half drive to the Cape.

Deb and Barney were glad to see me after my four day absence. My intent was to be gone for three days but I'd extended my stay another day because of the success I was having. I left the van loaded except for the artifact bags. I put them on my work bench still tagged and bagged next to the artifacts from my previous four trips to Hannibal. I saw right away that I was going to need a larger work bench as the collection was growing in number. As I switched the shop light off, I left them in the darkness they'ed had known for perhaps a hundred years.

After a few days of researching I identified the maker's marks some of the ceramics were stamped with. As expected, the confirmation of the era in which they were manufactured didn't coincide with your years at the home. The feeling of failure began to nag me again. Then...it hit me! First of all, it was a remarkable recovery effort. Furthermore, while some of the objects were only up to one hundred years old, they are still a representative sample of items discarded by all dwellers of that magnificent, yet humble home. The realization came over me as I cleaned away the layer of dirt from the ceramic doll/figurine torso. It reached

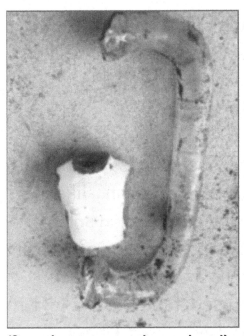
Porcelain torso and stein handle.

through the ages and touched me. The little girl who coveted the figure or the "house-marm" who admired it on a table are important too. Their stories, tho minuscule at this point, are being told and kept alive. They also help me. Anything they discarded after you left, Sam, is a signpost whether hallmarked or not. After your departure from Hannibal in 1853, the home was occupied as a residence by various people until it was declared that it was to be demolished in 1911, the year after your death. However, it was saved and opened as a museum in 1912. As late as 1937, a caretaker lived in the home and gave tours to fascinated "Twainiacs". I imagine I have some of the caretaker's trash in my collection. All things considered, an educational guess would be that I am digging the strata somewhere between 1884-1937. That's a wide margin but it's the best guess I can offer at this point, using the information of the hallmarks and charred bricks.

    With all of this in mind...I'm very satisfied with the dig so far. From this point, I'm looking forward to getting back to Hannibal soon after the break of spring. But for now, I ponder the artifacts and dream...   Hambone

185

Dear Sam,

Hoo-boy! Winter is back with a vengeance! Clouds, wind and brutal cold are the norm again after a few days of spring-like weather. My furry boy, Barney and me managed to get in some hikes along the river to look for artifacts exposed by erosion from the great flood of 2016. We did find dozens of bricks, broken bottles and ceramic shards from long ago used-tableware. I left it all in place for the next mudlarker to find. God knows I have enough of those types of items taking up space on my workbench in my shop. We visited the wreck-site for a bit, although I knew it was still underwater. The washed out bank above it is usually a productive spot to find stuff. We struck-out there also. It was good to visit the grave of the wreck, it is an old friend. I am looonnng overdue for a visit with Amy Elizabeth and secrets she has withheld from me for coming up on four years.

Whether I found anything or not, it was great to be back on the banks of the river. It's running swift and muddy. Trees of every size and sort are floating south along with items of man's trash. My imagination fires up and seems to sort out sights that are not true. The floating branches with their curled-up ends resemble fingers of corpses heading south. Steamboat disasters north of Cape Girardeau killed hundreds, as you well know. You knew many of the boats. Their charred cargos and victims were strung for miles down this great river. Boiler explosions, snags, groundings and collisions took their toll on souls and goods ascending and descending the Mississippi.

You had a somewhat short career piloting on the river. Your life was always in danger of being snuffed-out in a river disaster. While you survived the dangerous service to passengers, crew and cargo, I'm sad to hear your brother, Henry, was not so fortunate. His tragic drawn-out demise from the explosions aboard the steamer, Pennsylvania, June 13, 1858 was of horrific circumstances. Well over half of the passengers aboard went down with the boat. Those not killed immediately suffered on as Henry did...scalded, beaten and burned.

Thousands of wrecks litter the Mississippi River as a result of rich river trade over the centuries. As is expected, off the shores of Cape Girardeau are some fascinating hulks buried beneath the currents and mud. North of Cape is Devil's Island. This massive spit of land has been the end of many boats. The bend in the river is just short of 90 degrees to west preceded by a straight run that's delivered boats and cargo straight at the island and her shoals, snags and shallows.

The Union, side-wheel transport steamer, James Montgomery, snagged and sank off of Devil's Island December 11, 1861. A good sized boat, he was with a length of 270 feet and a beam of 36 feet. By 1867, the James Montgomery was declared a hazard to navigation by the U.S. Army Corp of Engineers after the steamer, Continental, struck it and sank followed by the steamer, Paragon...in 1868. U.S. "Snag-boats" removed James Montgomery in 1931. Ha...no hurry, I guess. No lists of victims exists from the three disasters.

Another Union boat was lost off the cursed island April 17, 1863. The steamer, **Alliance,** was stranded on the sandy, muddy riverbed. No casualties were recorded. The 144 foot, **Alliance**, was probably salvaged. I have to wonder what is left of her. They surely didn't recover every artifact!

Holding true to it's name, Devil's Island, claimed the **Rowena**, a side-wheeled Union Steamer on April 18, 1863. She went to the muddy bottom after a snag pierced her fragile wooden hull. No record of lost souls exists. **Rowena**, was 225 feet long with a beam of 33 feet. The 157 foot steamer, **John Stacy**, was snagged-off Devil's Island August 31, 1864. The **Stacy** was only a few months old having been launched in Cincinnati the previous June. There's no record of salvage or victims. More wrecks later, Sam. Life calls...

Hambone

Dear Sam,

Hellllo again! I know it's been four months since I wrote. Weather-wise, Spring finally arrived around a month ago. Ol' man Winter did not want to let go. Snow wasn't really in abundance and really cold temperatures were a rarity but cold temps and rainfall left me longing for warm sunny days. For the past month in Missouri, spring has sprung with oppressive heat and humidity it looks as if it will be constant for the next week or so. I've been slaving away opening pools to the level of exhaustion. Although I've cut my workload back by fifty percent, my advancing age and condition makes all efforts a formidable task. I will regain strength and endurance as the swimming season wears on.

There's so much going on that I want to tell you about, but before I get ahead of myself, I want to tell you about the remaining steamboat wrecks that lie off of our shores that I know of.

Collision of steamers, Tempest and Talisman.

One half mile south of Cape Girardeau, the steamer, Talisman, sank after a collision with the steamer, Tempest, on November 19, 1847, Talisman sank in ten minutes. Fifty one passengers and crew drowned in the frigid Mississippi. The crew of the Tempest came to aid the drowning passengers of Talisman as best they could. Local scoundrels arrived and chose to pluck as much floating luggage and cargo as was possible, avoiding and ignoring the pleas of drowning passengers. The engineer of Talisman refused to leave his post. He was last seen when the muddy water swept him back into the engine room to his death. A diving bell was used during an attempted salvage and recovery of victims. Only five bodies were recovered from the remains of Talisman. I have to wonder if you knew of Talisman and her fate as you piloted the bend dozens of times during your time on the river.

All hell broke loose when the steamer, Seabird, caught fire and exploded near the St. Vincent Seminary January 4, 1848. Due to ice flows, Seabird, was tied up along the shore. Part of her cargo was 1,200 barrels of gunpowder. By the time the fire of unknown origin was discovered it was too late. The captain ordered the crew to pull the plugs and scuttle her to smother the flames and avert disaster for the boat and sleeping townspeople unaware of the

Image of the Seabird. Photo: Perry Alt

wee hour emergency. The crew was unsuccessful in scuttling the boat.

The Captain and his men struck out to warn the town of the coming explosion. When the explosion lit-off, it was the loudest noise ever in this region of the country. The roof of the seminary was lifted upward several feet and settled back into place. Many of the startled and shocked people of Cape thought an earthquake had struck. Windows and doors of structures were blown inward for a great distance from the blast. Some prayed, thinking it was the second coming!! No deaths or injuries were recorded. As late as 1930, **Seabird's** remains were visible on the bank of the river. I imagine you saw it many times when ascending and descending the river through Cape.

The Union Army stern wheel steamer and ram boat, **U.S.S. Mingo,** sank accidentally on November, 1862. **Mingo,** was quite the warrior, Sam. She saw action at the battle of Vicksburg and the first battle of Memphis June 6, 1862. The final resting spot of, **Mingo,** is nearly mid-river north-northeast of the present day, Red Star Conservation Area.

Burning of the steamship Stonewall.
Image: Southeast Missouri State University Press

On October 27, 1869 the passenger Steamer, **Stonewall,** burned and sank upriver a few miles at

Neeley's Landing. During a game of cards, a candle was knocked over igniting a bale of hay. What should have been a minor incident turned out to be a tragic one. Without a bucket of water available to extinguish the flame, the fire quickly spread to other bales of hay. Panicked passengers began to jump overboard in order to escape being roasted alive. In an attempt to give his mostly drowning passengers a chance to escape, the pilot grounded Stonewall on a sandbar. Unfortunately, it pivoted into the wind causing the flames to wash through the boat bow to stern. The people of Neeley's Landing came to the aid of the stricken 250 passengers. Only fifty survived. Many of the survivors of Stonewall were taken-in by the citizenry of Neeley's Landing. Around sixty unclaimed bodies were buried in a mass grave; it's location now lost to the fog of history. More later....

Hambone

Message Forty-six...
"The Mel-Box"
June 30, 2016
Cape Girardeau, Mo.

Dear Sam,

I have fantastic news! Since I last wrote you, arrangements have been made for my return to Hannibal for some more digging in your yard. As it stands, I will be there July 10-14. I've spent the past few weeks preparing gear and making plans for the expedition. Last October during my drive from Hannibal town to Cape, my mind was swirling and scheming as to how to approach my next digging effort in 2016.

The October 2015 effort proved the hot spot to be a real honey-hole and not a fluke. But, to return to the dig using the same methods would be a foolish. It has to be sped up and also be conducive to good recording of data. Keep in mind the artifacts recovered came from three test holes, one foot square and three feet deep or as far as my hand and trowel can reach. My plan is to open up a section of earth roughly three by two feet, if not more, and dig as deep as possible into the trove of artifacts. Each shovel full of dirt will be passed through a screen-box I've constructed. This approach will be more efficient than laying on my belly and reaching into

The "Mel-box"

a hole, plucking out only one artifact at a time. The screen box I built has been given the name, "Mel Box", in honor of our great friend Mel Fisher. As you recall, the excavating tubes on the back of treasure boats are called, "Mail Boxes", due to appearance. Mel invented them.

While the plan is to be in Hannibal the tenth through the fourteenth weather has to cooperate. Too much rain slops up the dig and fills holes with liquid sunshine. Notebooks and gear get soaked. Metal detectors and hand held pin-pointers can be thrown off by the wet ground. Water seeping into the electronics of the devices can ruin them. On the other side of the coin, high temperatures and humidity, like we have experienced recently are also not desirable to work in. Such conditions wear an old man down causing me to take more frequent breaks from the task at hand. It is a big deal for me to plan, pay for and execute an expedition to Hannibal. I gladly provide the labor and expense. However, I want to excavate as much as possible. If the current weather pattern continues, I'll have to delay the trip. Disappointing? Yes! I'm optimistic the weather will be proper. In a few days the long term weather forecast will show me if I need to start packing gear and essentials or notify my friends of a delayed effort. We shall see. Most of the time I'm forced to delay at least once. It's usually rain that delays me. This time it could be the heat.

For the second straight year I'll be missing, "Mel Fisher Days", in Key West because I'll be in Hannibal. It's a yearly event celebrating Mel and the anniversary of the discovery of Atocha. Last year was the thirtieth anniversary. It was a bad one to miss. Many of my "Golden Crew" comrades were present. It turned out I

194

had to cancel Hannibal due to rain. I attended neither! ##^#%^# $^&...oh well. There will be many more, "Mel Fisher Days" celebrations in the future. I want to strike in Hannibal while the iron is hot. I'd rather be there. That's where I belong. Sam, the coming dig is going to produce more amazing objects. If I may dream a bit, an object will surface that I can trace directly to you. The refuse spot is loaded.

Once again I think of what you said about expectations..."A thing long expected takes the form of the of the unexpected when at last it comes." I will keep that in mind, Sam. I can be optimistic by not taking it as a warning...right?

If the weather is on my side, the next message will be written in Hannibal. There, I will toss this message into the Mississippi...

Hambone

Dear Sam,

A massive high pressure system lingers over the midwest encasing all of us in a nature-made greenhouse. Humidity hangs thick like airborne molasses and only shade makes outdoor activities survivable. The heat is oppressive to mind and body with the ground as hard as concrete featuring the carcasses of unfortunate earthworms that have dared to cross any span outside of their subterranean world. The cicadas are screaming and the frogs are silent in the creek. So goes the heat wave of 2016. So went my anticipated trip to Hannibal last week. And so goes any immediate attempt to dig the refuse pit under your old bedroom window at the rear corner of the house. Although I cancelled the expedition due to the summer's inferno, it turned out that in addition to the raging heat in Hannibal, severe storms rolled through that would have made excavating a muddy mess anyhow.

I am numb to being totally disappointed by the cancellation and the continued waiting. Treasure hunters know all too well about patience. Patience soothes the frustrations. Bottom line, self-assurance is as simple as the artifacts that have been there for ages...they're not going anywhere.

I will be sixty-two in a few weeks, Sam. The inferno outside drops younger men than me. To survive the environment, my work would proceed only at half pace. It's too far and the opportunity too rare to not work the dig as much as possible once I'm there.

So, I wait and tend to the rest of the full slate of my lists of chores and tasks. I'm treadin' water, Sam....treadin' water.

    With Hannibal on delay for awhile, my mind wanders south to the "Treasure Coast" of Florida. It's prime diving time for finding treasure from the doomed 1715 fleet. I'm supposed to be there now! Let's go, Sam. Mel is waiting...

                              Hambone

Dear Sam,

In the weeks since I last wrote, so much has happened. Some occurrences were hardships...some were victories. I guess the ratio between both categories were roughly a tie. The lowest point came when I injured my back while metal detecting on a century old baseball field at Capaha Park here in Cape. We had permission to work the entire complex before any coins or artifacts are buried by an overlay of astroturf. The repetitive motion of stooping and digging in the hard soil caused me to strain a ligament. I've been laid up in my basement man-cave for over two weeks. Two days ago I returned to light duty. It's great to be out of confinement even though my abilities are still limited. My 'ol dog, Barney, stayed at my bedside as I recovered. He's looking forward to escaping confinement when I'm up and about. We both need a good walk along the riverbank. He's become quite the "river rat" the past few years. The injury was the nail in the coffin of any hope of getting back to Hannibal this year. The screen-box I built for sifting artifacts from the soil of your home will have to wait until 2017 to be used. And used it will be! Great objects will be revealed by it's multi screened surfaces.

As promised, let's talk about the doomed 1715 Fleet's treasure wrecks off the east coast of Florida. Much like the Atocha, this fleet of ships met their end in a great hurricane on Wednesday, July 31, 1715, when at least a thousand souls drowned. For nearly two and a half centuries the remains and names of the

Dear Sam,

In, **"Mark Twain, A Biography"**, you are quoted..."Heaven goes by favor. If it went by merit, you would stay out and your dog would go in."

In a letter to William D. Howells, April 2 1899, you wrote... "The dog is a gentleman; I hope to go to his heaven, not man's."

In, **"Pudd'nhead Wilson's Calendar"**, you had this to say about our best friend..."If you pick up a starving dog and make him prosperous, he will not bite you. This is the principal difference between a dog and a man."

Dammit, Sam...nearly five months ago, on November 10th, Ol' Barney crossed over the "Rainbow Bridge". It was a peaceful affair as much as could be. He died in my arms in the familiar surroundings of his beloved deck off of our dining room. His Veterinarian came to our home to spare him a much hated trip to her office. When the hypodermic was inserted into his left front leg, he yelped just a little bit but immediately refocused attention on lapping up his favorite ice cream treat I'd provided for a distraction. Seconds after the chemicals entered his bloodstream, he slowly stopped lapping his last treat, sat bolt upright and stared directly in my eyes with laser beam focus. His eyes closed slowly and his head gently lowered into my lap. My sidekick of nearly sixteen years was gone.

As age does, it caught up with Ol' Barney. September and October weren't good months for him. His appetite was gone and he lost his mental and physical faculties at a rapid pace. In spite of more outings and an increased amount of leashed walking around the property, he rarely made it through the night without messing himself and his bed on the floor next to me. I felt the time was at hand to let him exit with dignity and **that,** he did. Knowing three days ahead of time of the fatal appointment, allowed him and me to make the rounds of all our favorite places on the river, at the lake and beyond. We did it all.

I had the old boy cremated. I spread his ashes at the end of the boat dock at the Elk's Lake...our favorite place to be. We made hundreds of trips to that place of escape to walk, fish and camp. It's given me some measure of comfort to know where his ashen remains are. Maybe someday, most of, if not all of my charred remains will join my canine friend at that serene watery grave.

His passing created a huge void and a pile of grief for me to sift through. I threw myself at many projects, performing with tear-blurred vision. We cruised to the Bahamas and flew to Jamaica. I started a new exercise habit by resuming my wintertime swimming. Along with the

Barney's watery grave

exercise, I ate better and lesser. Here I sit twenty pounds lighter and in better shape for activity and chores. One thing I couldn't do was to write. It took too much sitting still and thinking. Sam... I'm back and I am better.

Mid-May is the best guess I have for returning to your boyhood home. It'll be good to be there. One more hole....pat Ol' Barney's head for me...   Hambone

205

Dear Sam,

I have great news! Plans and reservations have been made and chiseled in stone for our lodging in Hannibal...and here we come! Deb and I will be there June 7th thru 12th. Only one factor looms to cause delay and rescheduling...adverse weather conditions. If rain soaks your yard in the days before our departure, I'll cancel. Returning to the artifact rich area of your old homestead is something I've waited on over a year and a half. It's impossible to dig in an oozy mess of mud efficiently. Enough of that. Anything else said about the matter may jinx it.

However, in this message, we **are** going to Hannibal. What I'm about to tell you, I've been sitting on for some time. This is another example of why I've sat here going on four years now, pecking at the keys for your attention. Hannibal itself, before and after your citizenship, is the subject of this latest correspondence tossed your way.

I tell you Sam, Hannibal...little old Hannibal, has produced a lot of notable achievers since its platting in 1819 by Moses Bates and its incorporation in 1845. The 15 square-mile city has produced citizenry who launched their lives there and went on to make a real difference in this world. Here are the most notable ones...

(1)...**Jacob Peter Beckley**...major league baseball player, (August 4, 1867 - June 25, 1918). "Eagle Eye" was his nickname. In 1971, Jake was inducted into, The Baseball Hall of Fame.

(2)...James Carroll Beckwith...(September 23, 1852 - October 24, 1917). His naturalist style of painting gained him respect as a giant figure in American art.

(3)...Margaret Tobin...(July 18, 1867 - October 26, 1932)

(4)...Robert Edward Coontz...(June 11, 1864 - January 26, 1935)... Robert was an admiral in the United States Navy. He sailed with the Great White Fleet and ascended to the title of, Second Chief of Naval Operations. Like you, Admiral Coontz was born in Florida, Missouri and moved to Hannibal. His parents were your neighbors and schoolmates at Florida.

(5)...Clifton Avon Edwards...(June 14, 1895 - July 17, 1971). He was also known as, "Ukulele Ike". Clifton was an actor, singer and a voice actor. In 1929 his hit cover of, "Singing in the Rain", made it to the number one position on the charts. He is very well known as the voice of, Jiminy Cricket in Walt Disney's, **"Pinocchio"**, released in 1940.

(6)...Lowell "Cotton" Fitzsimmons...(October 7, 1931 - July 24, 2004). Lowell coached the Phoenix Suns a few years and was twice named "N.B.A. Coach of the Year".

(7)...Lester Gaba...(1907-1987). Gaba was a renown sculptor and writer.

(8)...Clarence Earl Gideon...(August 30, 1910 - January 18, 1972). In the landmark Supreme court case, Gideon vs. Wainwright, our highest court ruled that a state must provide a defendant with a lawyer if one is unaffordable. Gideon spent time in prison for stealing fifty dollars in change from a juke box and a few bottles of beer. The court granted Gideon a new trial. New testimony convinced the jury to acquit him in an hour. He was forced to serve as his own attorney at the first trial.

(Bear with me Sam. I sense you are drifting. It's important I tell about your fellow notable Hannibalians! It gets good)...

(9)...Robert Vincent (Bob) Hogg...(November 8, 1924 - December 23, 2014). Hogg was a statistician. His textbooks are widely used in education.

(10)...William Powell ("Bill") Lear...(June 26, 1902 - May 14, 1978). Bill was an American inventor. He founded the iconic Lear Jet Corporation. During his four decade career he accumulated over one hundred patents. The 8-track cartridge was his innovation.

(11)...Warren H. Orr...(November 5, 1888 - January 12, 1962). Orr rose to be Chief Justice of the Illinois Supreme Court.

(12)...George Coleman Poage...(November 6, 1880 - April 11, 1962). George was the first African American to ever win a medal at the Olympics. In the 1904 games in St. Louie he won two bronze medals for the 200 and 400 yard hurdles.

(13)...Ron Powers...(November 18, 1941). Powers was an American Pulitzer Prize winning author for criticism in 1973, and was heavily influenced by you, Sam. Powers wrote, "**Mark Twain, A Life**", "**Dangerous Water: A Biography of the Boy who became Mark Twain**", and, "**Town Drowsing: Journeys to Hannibal**". In 2000, Ron co-wrote a New York times bestseller, "**Flags of our Fathers**". It won the, "Colby Award", the following year. His Pulitzer Prize was the first ever awarded to a television critic. His remaining body of works are too numerous to mention here.

(14)...Albert L. Rendlin...(April 7, 1922 - November 23, 2009), Judge Rendlin served as a Missouri Supreme Court Judge from 1977-1992. Albert was, Chief Justice of The Missouri Supreme Court 1983-1985. He served in the U.S. Army and saw action at, "The Battle of the Bulge", during World War II.

(15)...William Hepburn Russell...(May 17, 1857 - November 21, 1911). Russell was a lawyer and politician. In 1911 he owned, "The Boston Rustlers", a National League Baseball team. Early in his career, he was managing editor of three Hannibal newspapers. "**The Hannibal Clippard-Herald**", "**The Hannibal Journal**", and "**The Hannibal Courier**", Hannibal's contemporary newspaper. "**The Courier**", had several names over the years. You had this to say about the paper in a letter to the editor in 1908 recalling your tenure there as a youth, "**Printers Devil**", (type-setter).

"Surreptitiously and uninvited, I helped to edit the paper when no one was watching; therefore...I was a journalist. I have never been wholly disconnected from journalism since; therefore, by my guess, I am the Dean of the trade in America. I hope the

Courier will long survive me and remain always prosperous," Mark Twain.

(16)...Scott Sanders...(March 25, 1969). Sanders played professional baseball as a pitcher, 1993-1999. Scott pitched as a right hander for the San Diego Padres, The Seattle Mariners, The Detroit Tigers, and The Chicago Cubs...BOOOOO! He finished his career in Japan in 2001 pitching for The Nippon-Ham-Fighters.

(17)...Larry Dean Thompson...(November 15, 1945). Thompson served as Deputy Attorney General under President George W. Bush. He oversaw the cases against, ENRON.

There you have it, Sam. So many giants have sprung from Hannibal, AKA, "The sleepy little village". What an impressive list. There are more I'm sure. This list of notables will serve my purpose here. Recheck the list. Who stands out? Among these fine citizens of Hannibal, there lies a great connection between You, Mel, Hannibal, The **Titanic,** and a brave soul from your boyhood town.

I'll reveal it all to you in message fifty-two. It's time to hit the sack. We leave for Hannibal in two days. I'm loaded for bear at the "honey-hole"....　　　　Hambone

Dear Sam,

It's great to get back to you. A lot has happened since my last message. There's a lot to catch up on. The June 7-12 expedition to Hannibal went very well. If you could see the artifacts spread out on my workbench in the shop, (maybe you can?), you'd know what I mean. The refuse area under your old bedroom window continued to produce a variety of remarkable artifacts. It's like a spigot Sam. I am spoiled at the ease in which items appear in the excavation. Once again, I didn't cease the dig for lack of finds. The tap was still flowing. Debs and I left Hannibal out of time, energy and gumption. I was worn out, plain and simple. Before I get ahead of myself, let's continue the ending of message fifty one. In the next message or so I will fill you in on the recent Hannibal experience. What a trip!

Photo: Debra Barnhouse

In regards to all the famous people who called Hannibal home, did you study the list? Who stood out, making their inclusion into these floating "bottle-grams" a necessity?

Did you catch it? I reckon it's time for another shipwreck disaster to put it into perspective.

In a letter to William Bowen you wrote... "There is no unhappiness like the misery of sighting land, (and work), again after a cheerful, careless voyage." Your letter was written to Bowen just prior to sailing on the **Quaker City** in 1867. As you know, the destinations of the Holy Land and Europe gave you fodder for your best selling book during your lifetime, **"The Innocents Abroad"**. To this day, it's one of the best selling travel books of all time. If I may digress just a tad, it's impressive you had the guts to hop aboard another ship after the experience you had on the cholera-plagued, **San Francisco**, your last steamer voyage only a few months earlier which landed you in Key West. Okay...back to the shipwreck account. Sam, close to two years to the day after your departure with Comet Halley on April 21, 1910, the RMS **Titanic** struck an iceberg on April 15, 1912. Over 1,500 souls were lost. The opulent **Titanic** would've been your style Sam. Luxury and comforts afforded by the mighty steamer attracted the highest crust of society and her bowels were made available to hopeful immigrants coming to America. Just as the **Nuestra Senora de Atocha** did, **Titanic's** load of passengers represented

Image: Willie Stower

nearly every caste of society. While there are no records of acts of bravery during the sinking of Atocha and the rest of the 1622 fleet, there are accounts of heroism under personal duress as calamity struck Titanic.

Perhaps the most famous account of courage came from one, Molly Brown, aka..."The Unsinkable Molly Brown" The cries of, "Women and children first!" pervaded the decks of Titanic as the wounded ship sank bow first and began her death throes on her way to her grave 12,000 feet below the Atlantic, 350 miles SSE of Newfoundland. Some lifeboats fled the scene fully loaded with horrified passengers. Some of the boats left, half-full or less. Molly Brown refused to leave the ship. Instead; she insisted on corralling passengers into the lifeboats. Finally Molly was persuaded to board boat number six.

After lifeboat six made it away from Titanic, Molly insisted the quartermaster of the boat, Robert Hichens, return to the drowning sea of humanity and rescue as many as possible. Hichens refused for fear of boat six being swamped by panicked passengers coming aboard or by the suction of Titanic plunging to the depths. At one point, Molly threatened to chuck Hichens overboard. Accounts vary whether lifeboat six returned to the area and rescued anyone. Whether they did or didn't, Molly became a legend, an example of courage. Have you figured out why I ranted about Molly Brown, Sam? If

Lifeboat 6 approaching rescue ship Carpathia
Photo: National Archives

not, refer to the third person on list of notable "Hannibalians". Yes indeed, Molly Tobin was born in Hannibal on July 18, 1867. Her married name was Margaret Brown! Holy smokes, today is her birthday. I had no idea. Happy Birthday Margaret!!

This gets even better, Sam. Stay with me. I'm heading to bed. More in the next message. Wait till you hear it!

Hambone

Photo...Denver Public Library

Dear Sam,

Thirty two years ago today, Mel discovered the Atocha. Time passes so quickly. For me, almost half a lifetime has sifted like sand through my fingers since 1985. Tonight on my deck, I will toast Mel and all my former comrades of Treasure Salvors Inc. Today **was** the day!

I hate to keep you hanging. Let's get back to Margaret Brown, Titanic, Hannibal, and another amazing connection to Mel springing from all this. Here goes...When Robert Ballard, along with the rest of a Franco-American team found the remains of Titanic on September 1, 1985, he helped make the summer of '85 a historic, milestone-season of shipwreck discovery. Only forty-three days earlier, Mel's son...Kane announced to the world, over a crackling radio off Marquesa Island... "Put away the charts, we've found the mother lode"! In my opinion, Mel had pre-one-upped Ballard. While the news of Ballard's accomplishment went world wide, artifacts were not recovered until 1987. Mel was well into the documenting, salvaging, and bringing to the surface artifacts and treasure the world "ooh'd" and "aah'd" over. Meanwhile, Ballard didn't disturb Titanic. He left her untouched. The video, the stills, and the observations of the resting White Star Liner he showed the world were true treasures in themselves. Ballard eventually didn't get

215

his way. Later expeditions to the liner brought up artifacts of every sort for the world to see. I was lucky enough to view a slew of them at a traveling exhibit in Memphis and even purchased a chunk of coal from the debris field of the ship.

While the preceding paragraph shows us another great connection, it ain't the kicker! Fill your glass and light a cigar Sam. We're headed to the bottom of the North Atlantic. Men are in peril on a mission. It's the summer of 2000. After a two hour dive in the Russian Sub, MIR-1; a three man crew is mired-in only a few yards from Titanic's rust-crusted bow. As MIR-1 was approaching Titanic, despite due caution, it collided with the wall of sediment piled-up in front of Titanic. The ooze holding the sub in it's clutches was plowed-up when Titanic's bow impacted the seafloor eighty-eight years earlier. Pat Clyne, one of the three aboard MIR-1 in that predicament, recalled it for me recently. "We got stuck on our approach to the bow. We ran right into the mud-berm created by the ship's impact with the bottom. I guess we were there for at least twenty minutes before wiggling our way out." Whew...that surely must've seemed to be a lonnnng twenty or so minutes! I have viewed Pat's video from inside the sub during the ordeal. The courage reflected in their voices and manner is evident.

Pat Clyne and MIR submarines
Photo: James Sinclair

These inner-space explorers reminded me of our outer-space explorers and their demeanor while existing in an alien environment ready to snuff them out in an instant, whether it be equipment failure, or human error.

After their release from the mud, the crew continued surveying **Titanic** and collecting artifacts.

Two hours later, MIR-1 settled onto the deck of the legendary ship at Captain Edward J. Smith's ghostly bridge. Stored in a container outside the sub and accessible to the robotic-arm of the sub, was a special item to be delivered. The robotic-arm reached into the container. With delicate and purposeful motion, the rounded object was lifted out. Pat Clyne focused his video camera on the entire event. The item being deposited for all time is revealed in this quote from Pat. "I had Mel's ashes sealed in a small, clear acrylic bowl with a commemorative coin of his likeness made of bronze from the **Atocha**. I left it on the bridge of the **Titanic** in front of the steering column using a robotic-hand from MIR-1, the Russian sub I was diving on." **Pat continued...** "After thirty years of diving for Mel, I had become vice-president of his organization. I took the summer of 2000 on a leave of absence from Mel's company to join **RMS Titanic** on another adventure. **RMS Titanic** asked me to share what knowledge I had gleaned from Mel's judicial fight in his stunning historical victory in the Supreme Court of the

Memorial coin...
Sculptor: Don Everhart

217

United States that awarded him claim to the **Atocha**. I offered them all the judicial documents to defeat them...and they did. After RMST successfully won that right in the Fourth Circuit Court to salvage the artifacts of the **Titanic**, I was invited to join them on their next expedition... an offer I couldn't refuse. But, by that time... Mel Fisher had died of cancer after sixteen years of searching and finally discovering the "Motherlode" of the Spanish Galleon, **Atocha**".

Marine Archaeologist, James Sinclair was included in the expedition with Pat Clyne. Jim, along with Duncan Mathewson and Corey Malcom, was Mel's

Photo: Pat Clyne

principal archaeologist during the Atocha search before and after the big discovery in 85'. Yup, two of Mel's men were onsite at Titanic the summer of 2000, as was Mel. James Sinclair described one of his dives on MIR-1 for me this week. My question to James was, "During the dives, did you get to see Mel's memorial on **Titanic's** bridge?" Jim answered, "I was on dives that brought me to the stern and

A piece of coal from the Titanic

218

associated debris field. I never got to see where it was placed except on video, but...it was great that Mel ended up on the other of the two great ships found in the same year!"

Sam, to me...this was a remarkable moment in time and definitely a shared interest with any treasure hunter worth his salt. On the bridge, Mel was overlooking the scene from his impression stamped in Atocha bronze and his principal diver, Pat Clyne, doing what he always did best, searching for and recovering artifacts. Throw in James Sinclair's diving, recording, analyzing, and preserving artifacts...and it was a reunion of sorts. With a bit of imagination, the events were mirroring that summer of 85' when these men performed the same work on the Atocha.

Pat Clyne and James Sinclair
Photo: "Explorer's Club"

Molly Brown, Titanic, Hannibal, Mel, and you Sam; all linked together. Who woulda' thought? Pat Clyne's and James Sinclair's courage by diving into the abyss was as remarkable as Margaret Tobin Brown's on the surface during the disaster. Her coolness during the sinking of her ship was matched by Pat and Jim as they voluntarily sank in their submarines for science, curiosity, and to pay homage to their old friend and boss, Mel Fisher.

In message fifty-four I have some news for you. I hope it agrees. Heading to the river......

Hambone

Dear Sam,

In, **"Innocents Abroad"**, you wrote... "Travel is fatal to prejudice, bigotry, and narrow-mindedness, and many of our people need it sorely on these accounts. Broad, wholesome charitable views of men and things cannot be acquired by vegetating in one little corner of the earth all of one's lifetime," Sam; I'd like to add...travel delivers you to where you were meant to be, exclusive of what attracted you to journey, be it for holiday or business.

As I relayed in Message Fifty, after O'l Barn left us, we traveled to the Bahamas, Key West and Jamaica. In late April we drove to Sebastian, Florida to attend the "Treasure Hunter's Cookout", an annual event on the "Treasure Coast". I've been meaning to tell you what happened there. Damn Sam; all of the events, the twists, and the stories are back-logged. I reckon I should've told you this story sooner. It's the news I referred at the end of the last message...and it does affect us.

Unless you are in the "treasure-loop", the event's name, "Treasure Hunters Cookout", does not give justice to what it really is. Oh, make no mistake...it **is** a cookout! While there are many "Pirate Festivals" held annually which many treasure hunters attend, the "Treasure Hunter's Cookout" is more of a laid-back, intimate affair. For one day "it's ground zero" to the best treasure hunters on the planet; a mix of treasure hunters of both land and sea, along with their families. The range in talent among the people attending consists of folks who merely swing their metal-detectors in local parks, up to...hunters seeking the long sunken hulls of ships containing billions of dollars in bounty. All become one as ego's are checked at the parking lot. Throughout the day and evening, I'd say at least several hundred were in

Atocha Golden Crew
Standing left to right: Capt. R.D. LeClaire / Hambone / Capt. Syd Jones / Capt. K.T. Budde-Jones / Capt. Curtis White. Also, treasure salvors: Thomas Gidus and Bill Pearson
Photo: Jim Wilson

attendance. The sounds of laughter, stories being told and deals being cut emanated from the tables. As a matter of fact, I cut a deal using the tailgate of a pick-up truck as a desk. Captain Kim A. Ferrell had my contract ready for me to sign by prior arrangement. He also handed over to me my share of artifacts from the 2016 diving-season. For a fifth season with Captain Kim, I signed the dotted line and paid "me-pound-of-flesh" to become a diver/investor with him. By doing so, I'm guaranteed a percentage of the haul from the deep and can join the crew during expeditions to scour the ocean bottom seeking treasure and artifacts from the 1715 Fleet. After we shook hands, I told him I'd be back in a month to dive for a few weeks or more.

Now Sam, even though there was a lot of eating, swilling and revelry at the cookout, we were benevolent pirates. Proceeds from the cookout went to, "The Michael Abt Jr. Have a Heart Foundation". Michael was Mel's Grandson. He passed in 2006 at the tender age of fourteen from, sudden-cardiac-arrest. The foundation provides schools with AED'S that shock the heart back to a proper rhythm and hopefully, survival. Donations were offered-up, raffles were held and a good sum of money was collected for the cause. Before leaving the Cape...here in Missouri, for Florida...I bought a roll of raffle tickets in order to hold a cash raffle. My effort produced fair enough. The crowd of pirates opened-up their wallets and did us all proud.

Although the cookout was held hundreds of miles north of Key West, a handful of old crew-mates of mine from the Atocha days attended the event. It was great to see my seafaring comrades and to catch-up. Before I knew it, time was flying and it was time for me to work the crowd and sell a few raffle tickets. After an hour or two of collecting money and handing out stubs, it was time to draw the winning number for half the cash collected. I approached the podium fumbling with money, ticket stubs, and a parched throat. There was no room to set all my

Hambone awarding raffle proceeds to Nicole Johanson for the Michael Abt Jr. "Have A Heart Foundation" Photo: Jim Wilson

stuff down. A fellow and his wife whom had been entertaining us with guitar and percussion, along with their treasure songs, were set-up a few feet away. I asked the guitar-man if I could use his car seat as an office. My hands were full and I was too encumbered to draw the winning numbers. With a great North Carolina mountain drawl and a smile, he agreed immediately and offered any refreshment and assistance needed.

I drew the numbers and handed over the loot to the foundation and the lucky winner. I turned to introduce myself to the kind fella who allowed me to intrude on his stage and use his car for my possessions. I introduced myself. I was taken aback when he told me his name was Sam...Sam Milner. Immediately, I recognized his name. Sam is an accomplished song-writer, entertainer, author and publisher. I'd read one of his most recently published works a few months back, **"Unchartered Waters...The Life and Times of Captain Fizz"**. Captain Fizz is really...Carl Fismer, a living-legend of treasure hunting. Carl and Sam co-authored the book while Sam and his wife...Seajay,

published it through their company, **Sea Dunes Publishing House**. It's a great read.

When I told Sam about the messages I'd been sending to you, he seemed to show a genuine interest in reading them with the

Sam and Seajay Milner entertain the crowd at the "Treasure Hunter's Cook-out"
Photo: Jim Wilson

223

possibility of maybe publishing them in the form of a book! After stuttering a, "Yes", and swapping phone numbers with Sam, I told him I'd send him the messages completed so far for his consideration.

I had to make a hasty retreat to catch-up on a bit of rum, find Deb, and visit with old friends. Shortly afterward, folks began to load-up their things. Although the weather was magnificent all day, thunder-boomers and showers eventually threatened us. We were perched beneath the trees. If gold and silver attract lightning, this group of pirates were prime candidates for a bolt! Damn near everyone was wearing treasure-coin necklaces and shipwreck jewelry. We all said our goodbyes, vowed to come back next year and helped break down the encampment. The "2017 Treasure Hunter's Cookout" came to an end. What a fine time with the best of people it was!

Deb and I vagabonded farther south the next day and holed-up at Vero Beach, Florida. Our room was located on the beach by intent. Stepping-out the back door of the room onto the beach to metal-detect the sand and surf was pure joy. I didn't find much in the way of coinage, never-the-less...it beat digging the compact soil of the midwest.

Ever since meeting Sam Milner...coincidentally, another Sam... I thought about the idea of sending this manuscript to him. Hoo boy...was I ever torn! At best, I imagined these messages would someday be hand-bound, placed in a drawer, and most likely be forgotten. Maybe, at some point in time, they would've been read by family members and passed-on down the line as a communique from a long deceased ancestor. The concept of publishing still seemed far-fetched, especially since the act would require me to tell a few things about myself; not only to an accomplished word-smith like Sam Milner, but also...to anyone who might be plopping down a few bucks to read it. I put it all on the back-burner and thoroughly enjoyed the last few days of the vacation with Deb; fine dining...well, sorta...and brews by the sea.

After a few days we loaded the car and headed back to Missouri. It's always great to leave home, and...it's great to get back home again. We planned on a fairly quick two days of driving, or three, if the pace was too demanding. After traveling north all day, we blew a tire eight miles south of the Florida/Georgia border. With the help of a Florida Highway Patrolman, we resumed our trek. Deb and I laughed at the fact that at least we experienced bad luck during the trip's finale, and it was behind us. Well, those words came back to haunt us.

Sam, a few years ago I suffered a blood-clot in my leg. Between Valdosta, Georgia and Birmingham, Alabama the symptoms of a clot returned. My leg and ankle swelled! We holed-up for the night in Birmingham...350 miles from home. The plan was to either make a run for home the next day, or...head to a hospital. To make the story short, we did make it home. The end result is... I can't travel back to Florida in order to dive with crew on the 1715 Fleet because of my leg. I'm feeling a bit washed-up. Damn the luck.

Back to Sam, Sam. He liked the manuscript and had faith in my writing and story-telling. These messages will be published before the year is out. I'm planning on the publication date to be November 23, my Mother's birthday. Sam and I have been working together diligently for the past few months. So...we have guests now, Sam...and I welcome them. I hope this agrees with you. It was an unexpected turn. Nothing will change as we continue on. There's a lot more to tell you before we're finished. Or will we ever be finished, Sam? I don't know...

Hambone

Message Fifty-five...
"More Hannibal Pay-Dirt"
August 11, 2017
Cape Girardeau, Mo.

Dear Sam,

In message fifty-two I told you my darlin' wife, Deb and I went to Hannibal June 7th thru the 12th. The on-going dig at the refuse site was a continued success! I didn't give any details. In this message, I'll fill you in on the effort.

After days of planning, preparing and packing, Deb and I rolled out of Cape Girardeau late morning on the 7th. The weather prediction was holding steady at Hannibal. Although the temperatures forecast during the window of opportunity were well above my desire, no rain was expected. Knowing full well the temperatures were expected to be in the nineties, I borrowed a sun-shelter from Calvin Brennan. As usual, the Mississippi River driven-humidity was steady at inhumane levels. I had to have shelter in order to survive at the dig. The artifact-rich plot gets direct sun practically all day.

Shelter over dig-site

It was great to have Deb with me. Out of my half dozen trips to Hannibal this was her first time accompanying me. In the past, she had stayed behind at home taking care of Ol' Barn. I looked forward to showing Deb around Hannibal

227

Ham and Deb

and my work. Lord knows she'd heard enough about it for almost four years. It was time for her to witness it.

The drive to Hannibal was uneventful. We stopped every hour so I could walk around and stretch my afflicted leg. The plan worked. No swelling and no pain!

The first evening we walked down Hill Street from our lodging while we still had daylight.

Within five minutes we were perched under your old bedroom window staring at the area of interest where I planned to set up the sun-shelter, the "Mel Box", and all of my field-equipment in preparation for excavating. Hardly a scar was recognizable from my last effort in 2015. Only a slight small depression in the earth was noticeable where I'd refilled the test-holes nearly a year and a half ago.

Mel-box

228

Deb tugged my elbow, pulling me back to reality and said... "So...if you stare at it long enough do you think it's gonna' dig itself?" We laughed and then wandered on down to Main Street to one of my favorite eatery haunts. After a great meal and a few pops, we returned to our room and hit the sack early. Hitting the deck in the pre-dawn hours was essential! I had a lot to accomplish before one spade of "Boyhood Home" dirt could be turned. It was great to be back in Hannibal!

The alarm jolted me from my dreams before the dawn of the next morning had lit-up the sky. In a fog, I turned it off and wondered where in the hell I was? The sound of an alarm is something I'm not used to anymore. After a few seconds I realized I was in Hannibal and the clock was ticking. Within ten minutes I was out the door heading for the coffee pot in the lobby of our hotel. I dragged my feet out to the pool area, sat down at a table and watched the first light of the day reflect off the Mississippi. As I sipped the hot java, a few bats entertained me with graceful acrobatics under a street light as they neared the end of a nightly feast of skeeters.

After a definitive country breakfast and a few more cups of coffee, I drove my van a few hundred feet to your boyhood-home. Luckily, I was able to park a mere fifty feet from the dig-site. It took around ten trips to pack all the needed gear from the van to the refuse-site. The sun was up and the heat and humidity was climbing rapidly. I set up the sun-shelter first. It took some effort to do it by myself. After an hour of so of some cussing, a pinched finger, and re-doing the cantankerous-contraption, I had it in place over the refuse area and the "Mel Box". I was already soaked in sweat and a bit worn out. I returned to the van,

229

turned on the air-conditioner and regrouped as I slugged-down the remaining dregs of my coffee. Feeling a bit refreshed, I returned to the dig-sight. I referred to my field notes for measurements recorded in 2015. With a tape measure I marked-off the location of the previous test holes completed. I measured and staked-off a grid, 45 inches by 27 inches which overlapped the old test holes. Satisfied, I was set up, I carefully rolled back the green sod in order to open-up another window to the past. I muttered, "Today's the day!" While probing areas of the grid with a small rod, I felt resistance which made me glad. I wasn't surprised in the least.

Once I reached a depth of six inches my trowel began uncovering what I expected. Soon; pieces of broken ceramic, glass, coal, and other items appeared. The "Mel Box" performed magnificently when dirt was screened through it. I was well on my way to five days of probing, digging, tagging and bagging artifacts. Sure Sam...it was hot and gnatty doing the labor, but it was a heap more tolerable within the shade of the shelter and made any discomfort void by the task at hand. Almost every spade and scoop of dirt began producing artifacts of various nature.

Sam...I worked steadily and hard for five days. Although the temperatures and humidity were murderous, these old bones held out pretty well and I didn't strain anything. Energy-wise, I felt like a younger adult. The home and property have a charge to them, Sam, I must've tapped into it. That's all I can figure. Although I was spent after each day of digging and sifting, the next morning...I wasn't all stove-in, sore, or exhausted.

Goodnight Sam. I'll tell you all about what I found during the dig in the next message. I'm heading to the creek with a spotlight to see what critters are roaming past our home tonight. It's usually a menagerie of foxes, raccoons, coyote, deer (along with an albino), and who knows what. Along with the shrill of the cicadas and the bellowing of frog's, I'd say it will be a perfect Missouri Summer night at the stream.

Hambone

Dear Sam,

Today was an exceptional day! Today is Mel's birthday, **and**... we had a total eclipse of the sun. A hand full of best friends came over to celebrate and witness the experience of Sol's totality. For around a minute and a half, day became night and the heavens glowed with the corona of the sun, Venus and a few stars. I cannot

Columbus by: Camille Flammarion (public domain)

give it descriptive justice Sam. Did you ever witness an eclipse? If you have, I've found no record of it. In your 1889 work, **"A Conneticut Yankee in King Author's Court"**, you saved Hank from being burned at the stake by King Author's Court...with Merlin first in line, eager to stoke the fire! Time-traveling Hank knew of the coming eclipse of the year, 528. When Hank predicted the coming of blotting out of the sun, he was released to become a powerful man in the kingdom. Hank's "would be" executioners were convinced he possessed magical powers.

On March 1, 1504 Christopher Columbus pulled a similar stunt to convince Jamaican natives to continue provisioning him and his men. Columbus used the, Ephemeris of Regiomontanus, the German Astronomer (1436-1476), to predict the eclipse. It was Columbus's fourth and final voyage. Shipworms had decimated the hulls of his fleet. They were forced to beach on the north shore of Jamaica.

I tell you what, Sam. For the past sixty-three years the most amazingly impressive sight I'd seen was the Atocha and her cargo spread out on the ocean bottom. That sight was finally equaled today by what we witnessed in the sky! On Mel's ninety-fifth birthday no less! While you maintain a fascinating association with Halley's Comet, Mel...at least to me and folks that knew him, is now associated with the great eclipse of 2017. He would have been pleased.

Okay, back to the business at hand Sam. I promised to let you know what I dug-up beneath your bedroom window during the month of June. Dozens of shards of broken cups, plates, bottles, mugs and what-not were uncovered and bagged. Beautiful glazed-over artwork adorned some of the pieces of ceramic. Only one of the shards of ceramic bore a trade-mark and logo that made it possible for me to learn the period and history of the company that manufactured it. It was the Knowles, Taylor & Knowles Pottery Company in Sebring, Ohio. The company was founded by Issac Knowles, John Taylor and Homer Knowles in 1854. The company existed until 1931.

I found more pig or cow bones along with two teeth. The bones were neatly cleaved. What appears to be a two-inch pig tusk was mixed in with the teeth and bones. Out of the dig came another stein handle.

In one clump of earth I found a leather shoe sole approximately a size five. I can't say if it's from a woman or child's shoe. It's narrow, which leads me to believe it was not worn by a man. A spent ten-gauge shotgun shell with a brass rim presented itself on the screen of the Mel-Box. The inscription on it is not discernible enough to learn the manufacturer's identity and history.

What appears to be an intact inkwell bowl with the base broken-off was a fun find. I'm saving it for you. An intact bottle with inscriptions on the sides presented itself in the wall of the hole. The lettering on one side read, "Doctor S. Pitcher's", and on the other side read, "Castoria". Sam, on May 12, 1868, Samuel Pitcher received patent-number 77,758 for the medicine the bottle once contained. The concoction was a mixture of senna

leaves, bicarbonate of soda, wintergreen, water, sugar and extract of taraxacum. Other ingredients were pumpkin, worm seed, peppermint and 3% alcohol. Pitcher described it as a, "cathartic", or in simpler terms...a laxative. It's said the good Dr. Pitcher invented his Castoria in the barn behind his home. The bottle is hand blown. It's encouraging that it may be one of the earliest bottles that contained Pitcher's remedy.

One scoop of the rich Hannibal soil revealed the second clay gaming marble I've found in the dig.

Three small intact white buttons were found. If they'd once been part of a discarded item of clothing, it rotted away. The colors emitted by the buttons in direct sunlight caused me to believe they were punched from mussel shells.

What appears to be a two-inch piece of thick, black, drawing-chalk was found. I also found a thin, fractured piece of brick with mortar remnants still attached to it which could possibly be a chunk of chimney flu-liner. BAC in capital letters is stamped into it. The inscription

Ham inspecting a cup

is not complete. I have failed so far determining where, and by whom it was made. I lifted two intact bricks out of the hole. They are vintage. An expert dated them mid to latter Nineteenth Century. The remnants of a black comb with one intact tooth came out of

"The Haul"
Photo: Debra Barnhouse

235

the soil. What is left of it is three inches long. It's been melted by fire on both ends. I don't believe it's made of celluloid. Celluloid can suffer from celluloid rot and is extremely flammable. Besides not being intact and melted on the ends, no obvious degradation of the material is evident. It survived well buried beneath the earth for decades, if not a century.

To consider it to be made of contemporary plastic makes no sense. The first plastic combs were made in the mid-twentieth century. Considering the artifacts surrounding the comb, I feel sure I can say it predates the introduction of plastic combs. That leaves bakelite as it's composition, which was first formulated in 1907 by the Belgian-American chemist, Leo Baekeland in Yonkers, New York. Innumerable items, including combs, were manufactured using the remarkable replacement for highly flammable celluloid, until the advent of modern plastics.

Broken bottle-necks and bases were part of the bounty. The bases have only mold numbers on the bottom which do not identify the maker. A knob from a clear glass lid was saved also. I damn near cut my finger removing it. It sliced through my glove. I avoided injury.

I think that's everything I tagged and bagged during the effort Sam. Like I said, the refuse area was still producing when I had to refill the hole, break down the equipment and tidy-up the area. There's no doubt in my mind that hundreds of more items remain to be excavated the next trip. Barring rain, the next effort I've planned to be in Hannibal is September 28th through October 2nd. The plan is to continue at the same spot and establish the boundaries of the refuse-area. At this point I have no idea which quadrant of the rich area I've been digging.

Anything at anytime can appear. A treasure trove it is! Literally speaking, I have merely scratched the surface. The question remains: are all of the artifacts associated with the great "chimney-collapse"? If so, did a pit already exist where all the objects were tossed-in? If the pit did exist before the collapse, how old was the pit? What's at the bottom of it? Clemens' artifacts? The mixture of brick fragments and whole bricks certainly lend some credence to the "chimney-collapse" theory. However, it would make no sense to labor digging a hole to deposit the ruined items that suffered the calamity of the event. Simply wheelbarrowing or wagoning the smashed artifacts a few blocks to the river would have been much easier. I hope the pit, privy or whatever it is, existed before the "chimney-collapse". Burying the objects in an already dug hole was convenient. As it stands, that's the best I have to consider and go on. Along with all the aforementioned artifacts; pieces and pieces of plate glass, slivers, and rusty iron fragments filled my ziplock bags.

We threw Message 50 at Hannibal. It's contents pertain to Ol' Barney.

The presence of the melted comb and coal demonstrates hot ashes were discarded into the pit. On occasion, layers of ash are discernible in the strata of the walls of the dig. This helps me to rule out it being a privy. I cannot fathom hot ashes being dumped into an outhouse, especially so close to a home.

It was a hell-of-a-trip, Sam, and most satisfyingly productive. After digging everyday I'd stumble back up Hill street to the motel. After resting and showering, Deb dragged my ol' aching bones back down Hill Street to old downtown Hannibal for whatever itinerary she'd arranged for the evening. We saw a play on the riverfront that featured Tom and Huck reuniting in their later years.

One evening we witnessed a Mark Twain impersonator deliver one of your classic lectures. He did you justice Sam. It was well done. His eyes seemed to lock-in on me frequently as I sat there with remnants of soil from your home still lodged under my fingernails. It gave me chills.

We saw a pirate movie one evening at the cinema on Main Street, and explored America's home town while enjoying it's Twainesque ambience. One night we took a ghost tour and were handed dousing-rods to spook up spirits in the old cemetery.

Maybe I should acquire personal dowsing-rods and wave them around your yard during the next expedition! I've never given the rods any credibility, but it would be a hoot. Sam, may I take this opportunity to address the folks who have joined us. "Friends, I bid you to go to Hannibal at least one

Familiar faces visit the dig

238

Dowsing for spooks
Photo: Debra Barnhouse

time for a weekend. I guarantee you a splendid time and a memory-making event. Take it all in. Experience it. Relive it!"

What a day it's been Sam. An eclipse, Mel's birthday, and talking to you. I am beat. It's slap-up midnight. I know you'll enjoy message fifty-seven. It's a real corker. Que tengan buena noche, amigo...

Hambone

Dear Sam,

Today is another milestone day! The Atocha and the 1622 fleet met their demise 395 years ago today. The 400th commemoration rolls around in 2022. Having been born in 1922, Mel would have turned 100 just a few weeks earlier.

Sam, I have another story pertaining to the theme of all the parallels, coincidences and degrees of separation that weave themselves into history, especially when looking for buried treasure on land and sea. It's a very personal account. I think you'll like it, as well as the folks who have joined us. Here it goes...
In a letter to Will Bowen, dated November 4, 1888, you wrote...
"Both marriage and death ought to be welcome: the one promises happiness, doubtless the other assures it." If I may, I'd like to offer one of my few original quotes. It concerns matrimony..."Marriage is a wonderful state....I highly recommend it. You should do it many times." Both Deb and I are enjoying a second go around.

We were married August 12, 1996. Two days before the wedding, I was in dire straits. Deb planned on using her Grandmother's wedding ring. I was supposed to go buy myself one. Well...as you might have guessed, procrastination on my behalf produced no ring. I rolled out of bed on August 10 with the mission in mind of going to the jewelry store to complete my duty. As I shook-off the morning fog with a pot of stout black coffee, a memory came to me. In 1977 my Dad, Henry, gave me his wedding ring. He passed away the following year. It fit well enough, just a bit on the loose side. I wore it proudly anyway, especially after he died. In the fall of 1978 I lost the ol' man's ring while clearing out a small vegetable garden on my property! Search after search failed to produce the band of gold. I didn't have a metal-detector at the time. Time passed. In the spring of 1985 I sold the home, auctioned-off the furniture and packed my possessions in a travel-trailer along with my ol' dog Hobbit and three cats. We headed to Key West for a new life aboard the Denny Wayne and lucked-out by meeting Mel and salvaging the Atocha and Margarita....the ring was forgotten.

Getting back to the present...as I was getting ready to head to the jeweler an idea came to me. Why not make a detour and search for the ring with my detector? What were the chances? Time was short and our wedding was in forty-eight hours. But... just maybe...why not? I looked up the phone number of the occupants of my old home to ask permission to come search for the ring. Luckily the owner was home and gladly gave me the go-ahead. She told me they were having a family reunion, but to come on over anyway. I grabbed my detector and headed out the door. Deb asked me why I was going metal-detecting instead of ring-shopping. After hearing my plan I think she kind of rolled her eyes and told me good luck. I promised either way I would come home with a ring.

When I arrived at my old digs on Stoddard Street, sure enough...there were a number of cars parked and people milling around in the front yard just a few yards from the site of my old vegetable patch. To be honest, I wasn't thrilled that an audience was on hand to potentially get in the way or bog me down with questions about metal-detecting. It's usually fun to interact with curious onlookers when detecting. I was under-the-gun to get the search started. It was Saturday, the choice of jewelry stores plummets on Sundays.

I exchanged formalities with the land owner and her curious family. "Dog-day" humidity and heat were rising quickly, along with the infernal clouds of buffalo gnats that often accompany such conditions. I somewhat cordially avoided any further delay and approached the area of the old garden, now converted to plain grass. The crowd returned to their family revelry. I was sure some of them were rolling their eyes at my low-odds-effort to reclaim the family heirloom lost to the soil around eighteen years earlier. Okay, okay, Sam...I was being a little tight too. A "C-note" is a "C-note", right?

I muttered a half-ass, "Today's the day", and began detecting. Two hours into the effort produced nothing except the typical junk you find everywhere you dig. Nails, pull-tabs, bits of iron, aluminum foil wrappers and random denominations of face value coins wasted my time. Each hole I filled back in required time. Leaving the yard looking a mess was not an option. Since the plan was impromptu, my attire didn't help. My jeans and shirt were soaked with sweat. The onlookers approached me occasionally to see how I was doing and of course asked questions. I heard chuckling coming from the group at one point. I'm fairly certain they were laughing at some butt-crack I was exhibiting in my stooped digging positions. I pointed my rump toward an empty field next to the home as I dug the remaining holes.

Time ran out! No ring. There wasn't even enough time left to go home to shower and change. I would have been quite a sight to see walking into the jeweler's all stanky, sweaty, muddy-knee'd and grubby handed. I spit out a pesky gnat and cussed a bit. "The heck with it", I thought to myself. When you give up looking for treasure, that's when you try some more. One more hole..I gladly accepted a lemonade from a sympathetic witness and took a break in the shade.

A few minutes later I was back at it. One hole....nothing....two holes....nothing. Then, the detector let out a solid tone. I dug a huge divot of soil...this had to be the last hole. I broke the plug apart hastily. It was.....another damn piece of aluminum foil! I hung my head in defeat. As I looked down...Yarghhhhhhhhh!!! Gold in the hole, Sam! It was the old man's ring! I plucked it out and shot to my feet so fast I cleared the ground. I don't remember what I yelled out but I hope it was fitting for their family gathering.

I'm not sure who was more surprised, them...or me. They surrounded me congratulating and babbling on. I wiped it clean with my shirt tail and tried to put it on. Hoo boy, it was tight...but in fantastic shape. A little spit on my finger made it possible to slip it on. My fingers were a bit slimmer when I lost it.

As if all this wasn't amazing enough...a realization came over me. It was Dad's birthday!!! I had plum forgot about it because of my pre-occupation with the wedding. How about that! A second wave of excitement came over the crowd when I told them.

Within a half hour or so I was home. Deb about fell-over when I opened my dirty hand and revealed Pop's ring. We were married two days later on our back deck, AKA..."Deck Suds and Club". Her Grandmother's ring, and the ring my Dad wore when he married Ma in 1946 served their purpose.

Yup Sam, the parallels, coincidences, degrees of separation and just plain old unexplained eeriness weave themselves through every major discovery. That's been my experience. Oh, by the way...The detector I was using was made by Fisher. No relation to Mel, but still....Weather permitting, back to Hannibal soon. I am sending you four bottle-grams from there. The refuse area calls...

Hambone

Circa 1950. Mother: Bernice and
Father: Henry, and the old man's ring.

Dear Sam,

I noticed a quote in the 1923 edition of **"Mark Twain's Speeches."** *"No word was ever as effective as a rightly timed pause"*. Your quote applies mainly to lecturing and theatre, but also fits in with this message. Although the remaining letters to you contain a lot of action and thrills, our time is drawing near for pause. Before we part for awhile it's time to give you updates on progress with the historical sites we ponder.

The Cape Girardeau ship-wreck on the Mississippi River, the 1622 **Atocha/Margarita** shipwreck-sites near the Marquesas, the 1715 Spanish Plate Fleet wrecks off the "Treasure Coast", and of course your boyhood home all are being investigated to this day. In the coming years my work will hopefully continue in Hannibal and at the Cape Girardeau wreck-site. Maybe, next year I will be deemed fit enough to participate once again diving on the sunken treasures of the 1715 Fleet.

First, let's start with the Cape Wreck, **Amy Elizabeth**, aptly named after her discoverer, Amy E. Grammer. The river dropped to a level of eleven feet last week. The wreck was partially exposed for twelve hours. With my camera, I spent an hour with her. There she was, Sam! Months, if not a year, had passed since her last appearance. I was filled with relief. The great flood of 2017 did not cover over her bones with sediment to the degree I

245

feared. The stern-area of the riverboat was visible through the murky water and the large cleat was in place. Several of the deck cross-members were visible. Even though the river level was too high to do any real investigating of her remains, it was great to see her. In the wee hours of the following day she disappeared to slumber in the caressing current of Ol' Man River and the protection from the deteriorating effects of sunlight, air, and souvenir collectors. Someday, the conditions will come together in order to allow further study. Patience will pay. More data, along with the contents of its mud-filled hull will see the light someday. I'd like to be around to witness its final story and to contribute to it even more. When the river reaches the necessary level needed for more discoveries, you will find me there, as long as I am able to make the hike to her and to maneuver down the treacherous muddy and rocky bank.

Along Florida's "Treasure Coast", the salvage crews had a fair season bringing-up artifacts and treasure, with no reports of severe injury to crew members. The 1715 fleet is difficult and somewhat treacherous to work. Gold and silver coins were found in some number. Our crew of the Caribe, led by Capt. Kim Ferrell and Bill Black, did well. When the season ended in September their discoveries were numerous, though none of us can retire just yet.

Pottery, ships spikes, ballast stones and other artifacts recovered demonstrates they're on a trail of shipwreck debris and are relentless in their efforts. It's a big ocean, Sam. One huge haystack it is, with treasure representing the proverbial needles.

The Queen's Jewels could grace and glitter on the deck of Caribe in 2018. Even the best

Ham recovering treasure from 1715 Spanish Plate Fleet
Photo: Michael Fulmer

Captain Kim Ferrell surfacing with a four reale coin. Image: Bill Black

funded, well equipped and most capable of salvagers require a "luck factor". Luck, is what we need! It **is** coming! Hopefully, Captain Kim has another season left in him. Despite some struggles with his health, to say the least, Captain Kim fights through it all and is known to be out on the treasure trail when other salvage boats choose to remain in port.

The salvage of the Atocha continues-on as it has for the past forty-plus years. Captain Andy

Matroci leads the quest as captain of the **J.B. Magruder**. Captain Andy's experience working the site totals around thirty-five-plus years. He is this years recipient of, "The Mel Fisher Lifetime Achievement Award", which is presented during "Mel Fisher Days" in Key West. It made me happy to see Andy receive the honor and recognition of his achievements. A steady stream of artifacts were discovered by his crew during 2017, including part of a gold rosary complete with a mounted pearl, emeralds, silver coins and other pieces of the galleon. The elusive stern-castle of Atocha still eludes the divers. They will find it. Next hole....next hole...

Last, but not least, Hannibal and your boyhood home. Guess what? I went back last week! Everything worked out. I dug from September 28 to October 1. What a "dig" it turned out to be! I promise to fill you in on the next message. It was an amazingly successful effort.

I'm heading downtown to the riverfront. The Replica ships Nina, and Pinta are docked. A sight to behold they will be!

Hambone

Dear Sam,

Happy Columbus Day! I imagine some will be offended by the greeting I extend to you. It's true that Christopher Columbus and the Conquistadores who followed him devastated the indigenous people of the Americas as they pillaged, slaughtered, robbed and enslaved them. As they sailed from the "Old World" and marched onto the stage of the "New World", they utilized their superior weaponry. They also brought with them infectious diseases the native population had no defense against. I reckon if the natives of the Americas and the Caribbean had slaughtered or captured "pale-faces" arriving in winged ships, things would have been different. We know the rest of the story. For God, gold and glory, civilizations fell...an all-too-familiar story.

Each time Spain is awarded custody of a newly discovered treasure galleon by the United States and foreign courts, it is an injustice! If anyone is awarded custody of that wealth, why not the descendants of the indigenous people? I guess in a perfect world treasure salvors would be under contract with native peoples stretching from Chile to Canada in order to recover their stolen wealth while being fairly compensation for risk, resources and time. Spain deserves not one peso of the bounty!

Okay Sam, enough of that. I promised to tell you about our archaeological effort at your boyhood home September 28th through October 2nd. After a month of planning the Hannibal expedition, it all came together. Even the weather...the deciding factor, held in our favor.

Knowing full well some assistance with my effort would be handy, I enlisted the services of an old amigo, Dr. Vincent Powell. Vince and I go back almost thirty years. I looked forward to his company and his help. We laugh a lot and swap, mostly true stories. Since he lives in St. Louie, I picked him up on my way to Hannibal. When he threw his bags into the cargo hold of the fully-packed Atlantis Van, we "high-five'd" and went on our way. It'd been a long time since our last misadventure. We babbled and joked all the way to Hannibal. The compact disk, **"Mark Twain, Words and Music"**, made for great traveling tunes. The recording is a compilation of oration and music, telling of your life story. Various world renown artists lent their musical talent to produce it. The proceeds directly benefit your boyhood home. The songs helped us focus on our soon-to-come immersion into Hannibal Town.

After checking into our lodging, we walked down Hill Street to your home. I was pleased to find the outline of the grid made from my June expedition was barely noticeable. A fair stand of plush grass covered it. As we descended Hill Street, we continued along making a right on Main Street. In no time we were seated at a table on the sidewalk and dining at my favorite watering-hole and quaffing a few dark beers. After we chowed-down, there was enough daylight left to set up the dig-site in preparation for cracking the soil the next morning. With Vince's help, set-up was a relative breeze. The sun-shelter, Mel-Box, assorted tools, wheelbarrows, buckets and all the what-nots were in place when we went back to the hotel.

After coffee and breakfast the next morning, we drove to your home. Although we'd set up the main bulk of the gear, there were other tools and devices which we needed for our work still stored in the van. I measured out a new grid overlapping the previously dug grid by a few inches. With trowel in hand I began rolling back the grassy turf to expose bare earth. Over my shoulder I heard Vince say..."Today's The Day!" In my state of excitement, I'd forgotten to say it. I replied to Vince, "You got that right brother. Today's the day!"

Digging commenced as big Vince stood ready to run dirt through the Mel-Box. After a half hour of scraping and handing up buckets of dirt to Vince, nothing popped up. Due to the drought, the ground conditions made the earth as hard as concrete, three quarter cured. I wondered if I'd jinxed myself by telling Vince that we'd start finding artifacts immediately at the "honey-hole". Thoughts of relocating the grid began to nag me. Hopefully, my whispered expletives didn't reach the ears of passing tourists and their families. At least the temperature was perfect, unlike the 100-plus heat index during the digging in June. I stayed at it.

Dr. Vincent Powell

251

Finally, a few small pieces of glass shards and ceramic bits appeared first. In the middle of the grid I decided to excavate a four-inch wide core sample. Four inches down into the effort large pieces of ceramic shards, square nails and encrusted iron fasteners appeared. Eureka...we were on it! The refuse area again turned on a spigot of objects. As I expanded the test-hole to encompass the rest of the grid, Vince got busy working the sifting screens. Whatever treasures got past me in the buckets appeared before him as he meticulously examined the spoil dirt. For the remainder of the trip we tagged, recorded and bagged a continuous flow of discoveries. Yes Sam, the very things we are accustomed to came out of the dig: broken plates, cups, bowls, fasteners, coal, fragmented brick, glass, broken bottle necks, beautifully colored pieces of porcelain, square nails and suspected pig bones.

On the second day a heavily oxidized, yet sturdy, Missouri Mule Shoe complete with a chunk of coal imbedded in the top of it's forward arch was revealed! Also, three more clay gaming

marbles, intact bottles, an ornately flowered ceramic lid, the end of a wrench, four more buttons, strips of leather with lace holes (probably from the shoe sole I found in June), an oval eyeglass lens, a large copper lid, a one inch by one inch quartz cube, a small broken brass fitting and a spooky looking small chip of porcelain with a partial face.

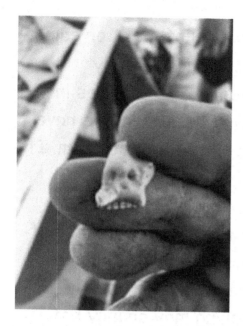

Only the nose, a nostril and teeth survived. It was creepy.

On the third day of excavating I was busy scraping dirt when over my shoulder Vince exclaimed, "We have a coin!" I thought... "Surely not"...as I jumped up to take a look-see. Buttons can mimic-coins when patina and crud cakes them. Vince handed me the

Uncleaned Nickel

round object. I studied it but the shade beneath the shelter hampered my evaluation. I stepped into the sunlight with the possible first treasure-coin found in the dig. Heavy greenish patina covered it. I saw writing and signs on it. My pulse quickened as I raised the object to my magnifying glass. I'll be damned, Sam...it was a coin and it was old! I poured water over it to help bring out more detail, avoiding the

Example of a shield nickel

temptation to rub it and risk damaging it. It was a "shield nickel"! It was designed by James B. Longacre and was produced by the United States Mint from 1866-1883. You left your boyhood home in 1854. I cannot attribute the nickel to you or your family. Finding the coin was

253

as big a thrill as finding Atocha/Margarita pieces of eight or coins from the 1715 Spanish treasure fleet. The find was totally unexpected in the refuse area. It's a possibility the coin was in the pocket of a discarded piece of clothing. The buttons we have recovered could have belonged to the garb the coin came from. It was great to find a treasure coin!

During the last day of digging, another round object appeared that looked like another coin. It was fused to a piece of scrap iron. Further examination of it lends me to believe it is a metal button. No detail appears on the face of it and it seems to have a slightly convex surface. Careful cleaning may or may not reveal it to be a coin. Whether a button or coin, the object is unique since it is bonded to the piece of iron. It will remain that way. I won't separate the two.

We spent our down-time bicycling around Hannibal. We tossed three bottles into the river during the time we were there. Hannibal was really busy in the historic downtown area of town. One thing I've noticed is that Hannibal is really dog-friendly. Curs of every size and shape stroll along with their owners and grace most outdoor eateries, lurking under the table for random dropped scraps and offerings from their masters. I thought a lot about Ol' Barney. He's been gone almost a year. Too bad he never made it to Hannibal. I miss my sidekick.

Yup, Sam...overall it was one of the best digging efforts ever. I'm finished until 2018. I'll have a busy Winter as I research the new finds and recheck the entire collection. When I return to the dig next year I plan on handing over all the artifacts to the director, as well as the site-map, drawings, images and provenance of the items uncovered so far. A comprehensive report will top it all off.

Optimism rules as I consider finding an artifact attributable to the Clemens' family. Maybe next year. The next grid we work could contain that ultimate prize. You gotta believe it.One more message is floating your way, Sam. Until then...

Hambone

Unique artifacts from the dig in Hannibal

Dear Sam,

From **"Mark Twain's Own Autobiography"**, (North American Review, Feb.1, 1907), you had this to say about practical jokers...

"When grown-up persons indulge in practical jokes, the fact gauges them. They have lived narrow, obscure and ignorant lives, and at full manhood they still retain and cherish a job-lot of left-over standards and ideals that would have been discarded with their boyhood if they had then moved out into the world and a broader life."

Hannibal

As he slipped into the courtyard of your boyhood home a few weeks before my July 30, 2012, first ever expedition to Hannibal, the man was a bit nervous, yet smug, as he contemplated what he was about to pull off. It was broad daylight and his mission was to "get me", and to "get me" good! This old friend of mine knew of my plans to metal-detect the property. He had driven well over a hundred miles in order to deliver a mystery to me.

Palmed in his hand were five freshly red-lettered quarters. The coins spelled out, R-A-N-D-Y! As he strolled around the grounds of the property, occasionally he stopped and pushed each quarter into the earth, using a ruse of tying his shoe or admiring the immaculately trimmed flora surrounding the area. Once his mission was complete, he beat a hasty exit undetected and returned home. I can imagine the smirk on his face as he imagined me finding the coins spelling my name.

It's true, Sam. The quarters spelling out D A Y were planted by one of my friends to prank me! I have to say, "Bravo", to him. It was the best I've been fooled in my entire life. Talk about going out of your way to pull a caper! He fessed-up recently. I was shocked. I was agitated. I was amused. A gamut of reactions came over me. But in the end, who was the prank really on, me or him? If I hadn't found the three coins spelling out D-A-Y, would my senses had been keened to being on the lookout for other parallels and coincidences allowing a conversation with you and tying together every major historical site I've investigated and dived on? Would we even be having this conversation? What are the odds of me finding the ones I did...instead of Y-D-N or any other combination? I've been all over the grounds with my detector. Where are the coins lettered R and N? To me it's as astounding as the original story...when their origin was a mystery. I thank him for planting the coins to shock me. But, I will get him back. It will be epic. It starts now. I will leave his name a mystery for the first part of the payback. Your quote about practical jokers was a good start.

Earlier tonight I stepped outside to have a cup of coffee and gaze at the night sky. It's a windy, fresh Autumn evening. Storms are blowing-in early in the morning. My interest in the heavens tonight is more than usual. Earth is passing through the debris left behind by Comet Halley! How apropos it is for the meteor shower, Orionid, glittering the night sky as we close out our written communication for the time being. The name of the shower reminds me of your brother, Orion. The meteors are the remains of Halley's dusty tale.

What about the great comet itself? A few minutes ago I checked it's present location. As we speak, Halley is still traveling away from the earth and sun. It's distance from us at present is 5,198,180,042 km, or around 3,229,999,330 miles, traveling at 64,871 mph! Only a few telescopes are able to pinpoint Halley's location in the constellation Hydra. The last time Halley was visible by telescope was in 2003, seventeen years after it's last visit with us. Humankind will be dazzled when Hally appears in the night skies again around July 20, 2061, the 76th anniversary of the discovery of Mel's, Atocha.

Sam, besides the circumstances of the red lettered quarters prank, everything I shared with you over the past four-plus years is the truth of my best recollection. A few times I might have gotten a bit dramatic, but I guess the intensity of a writer varies with the passion felt by different circumstances and stories remembered. After other readers joined us, I had to convert all of our original bottled messages into book form. What a task it was! I had good help though from publisher, Sam. A worthy labor it was, including the pictures rounded-up and added.

As I told you many messages ago, hopefully I have demon-strated with the Cape Wreck and with the effort in Hannibal treasure hunters and archaeologists can work together for the benefit of each other, as well as for a public interested in history and the artifacts associated with it. The final reports, cataloging, maps, images and the artifacts will be submitted to the administrators of your boyhood home. Hopefully the collections will be seen, enjoyed, and when possible, held by many appreciative people.

Of the sixty bottled messages thrown over the years only three have been found and reported back to me. As you know, two of the letters were found in extraordinary circumstance. One was was a humdrum discovery with no real coincidences revealed. My hope was for more to be found before we end here. With the rise and fall of the river I wonder where they have ended up. Some are buried under the sediments in farmer's fields and along the banks of the Mississippi River. A few have experienced a shattered end on rocks or whirling propellors. Maybe some of the messages made it to the Gulf of Mexico and the open sea. Most, may never be found. It might take a few more weeks or up to a hundred-plus years for some to be discovered. The bottles are sealed well. Perhaps, in the distant future one will be found. The finder will be able to look this book up in the Library of Congress, if the interest is there.

Once I read, "The hardest thing concerning writing about Mark Twain is finding a place to stop. You have to pick a point and end it." It's the truth, Sam. In almost every message I've written to you, I could've written different accounts, parallels and coincidences. I had to cherry-pick the best of the best. So much remains unwritten. Mel Fisher is in the same category. I've only scratched the surface on both of your lives. At times, I've felt presumptuous for making the effort. Hopefully, folks will be kind to me and enjoy what I've committed to paper.

Off I go, Sam. I will continue the digs at the river wreck and Hannibal next year. Notes, I will keep. Images, will be taken. And bottles, will continue to be flung! We will get to the bottom of our inquiries! Somewhere on the boyhood home property is a trace of you. I will not give up. Part of my future will be that of a book seller to anyone interested in what we have accomplished here. I look forward to it, and...sailing my 1963 sixteen-foot Falcon sailboat. I've been restoring it for the past couple of months.

You left so much behind for us, Sam. It's been my pleasure to write something for you in return. It's time someone did. If I make a few bucks from the book, some will be donated to the preservation of your boyhood home. Maybe I should earmark it for grounds-keeping! Ha.

Until next time, Sam...please toss a stick for my 'ol boy, Barney, and remind him to meet me at the Rainbow Bridge...

Hambone

Deo and Mel Fisher...Photo: Carol Tedesco
"Once you have seen the bottom paved with gold, you'll
never forget it."

Samuel and Olivia Clemens...Photo: public domain. "There comes a time in
every rightly-constructed boy's life when he has a raging desire to go
somewhere and dig for hidden treasure." (The Adventures of Tom Sawyer)

SUGGESTED READING LIST

"**Atocha Treasure Adventures; Sweat of the Sun, Tears of the Moon**"... A True Story by Captain Syd Jones.
Publisher: Signum Ops, 2011

"**The Dream Weaver**"... The true story of Mel Fisher and his Quest for Treasure of the Spanish Galleon, Atocha. By Robert Weller
Publisher: Fletcher and Fletcher Publishing, LLC. 1996

"**Fatal Treasure**"...by Jedwin Smith.
Publisher: Wiley; John Wiley and sons Inc. 2003

"**Treasure**"... by Robert Daly.
Publisher: Random House, 1977

"**Discover Archaeology**"... by George Sullivan
Publisher: Doubleday, 1980

"**Aztec**"... by Gary Jennings
publisher: Atheneum, 1980

"**The Rainbow Chasers, in the great Florida treasure Hunt**"... by Tommy Gore, as told by T. L. Armstrong.
Publisher: Signum Ops, 2006

"**Deadly Path To Treasure**"... A DVD by Robert C. Moran.

"**The Atocha Odyssey, The Life and Legacy of a Treasure Hunting Family**" by Pat Clyne.
Publisher: Terrel Creative. 2010.

"**Treasure Hunt, The Sixteen-Year Search for the Lost Treasure Ship Atocha**"...by George Sullivan.
Publisher: Henry Holt and Company, New York. 1987.

"**True Stories of Sunken Treasure, The Best of Bob "Frogfoot" Weller**"... by Bob Weller.
Publisher: Crossed Anchors Salvage". 2005

"**Treasure of the Atocha, A Four Hundred Million Dollar Archaeological Adventure**"... by Duncan Mathewson III. Foreword by Mel Fisher.
Publisher: Pisces Books, E.P Dutton, New York

"**Treasure Coins, of the Nuestra Senora de Atocha & The Santa Margarita**"... by Carol Tedesco.
Publisher: Sea story press. 2010

"**Mark Twain, Words and Music**"...A compact-disk. Through oral presentation and music, Samuel Clemens' life is portrayed. All profits from this remarkable work go directly to the preservation of "The Mark Twain Boyhood Home" in Hannibal, Missouri.
Produced by Carl Jackson and Cindy Lovell. Luke Wooten Station West Studio, Nashville, Tennessee.

Read anything written by Samuel L. Clemens!

Acknowledgements

I take this opportunity to thank those who have helped me during the writing of this book, along with everyone who has assisted me in the investigation of the historical sites covered in this book. I run the risk of leaving someone out, but I will give it my best.

Thank you Dr. Randall Rhodes for your encouragement to start the book and complete it. Dr. Rhodes read the succession of messages as they were produced for the past four years. His constructive criticism and genuine excitement with the book motivated me to keep going.

Thanks to my wife, Debra, who has been behind me 100% during every phase of this effort; whether proofreading, spending nights alone when I was locked in my office writing, or when I was in Hannibal metal-detecting, and excavating the amazing dig at the Mark Twain Boyhood Home.

I thank everyone who assisted me at the wreck-site of the Amy Elizabeth in Cape Girardeau, Missouri; whether your role was measuring, image taking, drawing, reporting on or being a safety presence in case of me being injured and alone in that isolated location. You have made a contribution to the knowledge and preservation of our great river heritage.

Thank you to the U.S. Army Corp of Engineers for the clearance to work the "Cape Wreck", and the Missouri Department of Natural Resources for allowing me some latitude while investigating the wreck. The DNR is responsible for historic wrecks and the permits to salvage them in our state waters. We have worked very well together.

I wish to thank my world class archaeology friends: James Sinclair, Dr. Corey Malcom and Dr. E. Lee Spence. Thank you for having been so helpful to advise me when questions arose as to how to proceed with many tasks. We have worked very well together and collaborated with the goal in mind of proper excavation and preservation of sea and land sites. That, we have done here.

Thanks to Sam, Seajay and Nan Milner at Sea Dunes Publishing House, as well as their publishing partners, Boots and Tina Atkins, for their encouragement and beyond-the-call-of-duty editing and publishing of my work.

Thank you to Dr. Cindy Lovell and Henry Sweets, past and present directors of the Mark Twain boyhood home, for trusting and allowing me to investigate and dig on the grounds of the home.

Than you Will Rogers for notifying me of the initial opportunity to metal detect at the Mark Twain boyhood home.

Thank you, Samuel Clemens, for the treasured literature you left behind, and to Mel Fisher for literal treasure and the knowledge being gained still today as a result of your discoveries which came with great personal tragedy.

Thank you Captain Curtis William Erling White for being my principal dive partner on the Atocha and Margarita wrecks, and for helping me become a diver for Mel's Treasure Salvors Inc.

Thank you Russell and Amy Grammer for inviting me to investigate the "Cape Wreck", Amy Elizabeth.

Stacey Wright and
Lester Goodin

Randy Barnhouse and Mel Fisher
1986 Photo: Crew

Digging at the Mark Twain
Boyhood Home
Photo: MTBH

Investigating another riverboat
wreck north of Cape Girardeau,
Missouri, 2012
Photo: Calvin Brennan

Atocha Expedition 1988

Guest bottle-thrower: Melissa Wade

Guest bottle-thrower
Steve Gerard

Guest bottle-throwers, the
Halbrook sisters: Jeanne, Jill
and Suzette
Photo: Debra Barnhouse

Guest bottle-thrower:
Dr. Randall Rhodes

Clemens family plot

Lester Goodin as Mark Twain
Photo: Stacey Wright

Riverboat wreck, "Amy Elizabeth"
fully exposed

Salvage boat Virgalona...1985

Artifacts and site map

Samuel Clemens and
Hambone at flood-wall, Cape
Girardeau, Missouri

Lester Goodin and Hambone
Photo: Stacey Wright

Randy (Hambone) Barnhouse

Randy Barnhouse is a retired teacher and has been a treasure hunter/finder for thirty-five years. His treasure hunting career began in 1985 when he was a member of the "Golden Crew" of Mel Fisher's, Treasure Salvors, Inc. As a member of the "Golden Crew", Randy helped salvage the treasures and artifacts of the Spanish galleon, Nuestra Senora de Atocha and her sister ship, Santa Margarita. Randy has also dove on other shipwrecks such as the Spanish 1715 treasure-fleet which lies off shore of the "Treasure Coast" of Florida. He has also excavated historically important land sites such as the boyhood home of Samuel L. Clemens.

Randy and his wife, Debra, reside along the Mississippi riverfront in Cape Girardeau, Missouri. Currently you will find him working on historical projects, educational consulting and sailing the lakes of Missouri.

"Now and then we had a hope that if we lived and were good, God would permit us to be Pirates." - Mark Twain

Made in the USA
Columbia, SC
13 February 2018